The Dark Man

The Dark Man

Deborah Wells

BOOKS

Winchester, UK
Washington, USA

First published by O-Books, 2010
O Books is an imprint of John Hunt Publishing Ltd., The Bothy, Deershot Lodge, Park Lane, Ropley,
Hants, SO24 0BE, UK
office1@o-books.net
www.o-books.com

Distribution in:	South Africa
	Stephan Phillips (pty) Ltd
UK and Europe	Email: orders@stephanphillips.com
Orca Book Services Ltd	Tel: 27 21 4489839 Telefax: 27 21 4479879
Home trade orders	Text copyright Deborah Wells 2010
tradeorders@orcabookservices.co.uk	
Tel: 01235 465521 Fax: 01235 465555	ISBN: 978 1 84694 293 8
Export orders	Design: Stuart Davies
exportorders@orcabookservices.co.uk	
Tel: 01235 465516 or 01235 465517	All rights reserved. Except for brief quotations
Fax: 01235 465555	in critical articles or reviews, no part of this
	book may be reproduced in any manner
USA and Canada	without prior written permission from the
NBN	publishers.
custserv@nbnbooks.com	
Tel: 1 800 462 6420 Fax: 1 800 338 4550	The rights of Deborah Wells as author have
	been asserted in accordance with the
Australia and New Zealand	Copyright, Designs and Patents Act 1988.
Brumby Books	
sales@brumbybooks.com.au	A CIP catalogue record for this book is
Tel: 61 3 9761 5535 Fax: 61 3 9761 7095	available from the British Library.
Far East (offices in Singapore, Thailand,	
Hong Kong, Taiwan)	
Pansing Distribution Pte Ltd	Printed in the UK by CPI Antony Rowe
kemal@pansing.com	Printed in the USA by Offset Paperback Mfrs,
Tel: 65 6319 9939 Fax: 65 6462 5761	Inc

We operate a distinctive and ethical publishing philosophy in all
areas of its business, from its global network of authors to
production and worldwide distribution.

CONTENTS

Acknowledgements   viii

Introduction   1

Chapter 1 The Dark Man   6
A typical dark man experience; Storytellers, mythographers, poets and psychologists: explaining the dark man; Models of understanding

Chapter 2 Meeting the Dark Man   26
What the dark man looks like; What the dark man is associated with; Where we find the dark man

Chapter 3 The Underworld   53
Where is the dark man found? What is the Underworld? What the Underworld contains; The passage through the Underworld; What lies on the other side?

Chapter 4 The Lord of the Underworld   75
The first encounter; The threshold; While passing through; The return; Why the dark man does what he does

Chapter 5 Introducing... Us   121
The dark man's relationship to us; What we should do when he arrives; What we should do while travelling through; What we should do at the other side; Do we have a choice?

Chapter 6 When It Goes Wrong   161
Interrupting the flow; Putting things right

Conclusion Walking with the Dark Man   182

Notes   190

Colin, Jack and Sam

Acknowledgements

My greatest love and grateful thanks go to my husband, Colin, and our two wonderful, handsome, amazing sons, Jack and Sam. Also, love and thanks to my dad, mum and stepdad John, to my brothers, Chris and Dan, and to my irrepressibly lovely nephew, Jamie. Thanks also to Crackerdog for his enduring canine companionship.

To all my friends, so very many of whom have shared their stories with me, thank you.

Thank you to John Hunt and everyone at O Books who have helped to make this possible.

Thanks to Dominique Shaw of York Place Studios for her wonderful photographs.

A thank you should also go out to the dark man and the other 'old gods' in heaven for, at the very least, making life so much more colourful.

I would also like to acknowledge my extraordinary grandma, René, and my lovely sister-in-law, Catherine, both of whom passed away while this book was being written. You will never be forgotten.

Introduction

There are more things in heaven and earth, Horatio,
Than are dreamt of in your philosophy.
Shakespeare, *Hamlet*, act 1, scene 5, line 166

Now, my own suspicion is that the universe is not only queerer than
we suppose, but queerer than we can suppose...I suspect that there
are more things in heaven and earth than are dreamed of, or can be
dreamed of, in any philosophy.
J.B.S. Haldane, mathematical biologist, 'Possible Worlds',
Possible Worlds and Other Essays (1927)

Have you ever woken in the night feeling certain that someone,
or something, was watching you from the shadows? Have you
ever dreamed of a terrible dark assailant, the memory of whom
you were unable to shake for a considerable time? Have you seen
a dark shadow flit from view while you were driving or when
you entered a room? Are you afraid of the shadows, or change, or
the unknown dangers that may be lurking down the road? Are
you lost and alone in the darkness and simply looking for your
way home?

Since the beginning of time human beings have been haunted
by a mysterious dark presence. It typically (though certainly not
always) takes the form of a tall, gaunt, dark man. It is usually
perceived as mysterious, loathsome or downright terrifying.
And it stalks us through our dreams, our waking lives and our
creative endeavours.

Through the ages this presence has been known by many
different names. However, today, it is often just called 'the dark
man'. And we have only to scan the history of religion,
philosophy, art and literature to see just how pervasive the dark
man really is.

Furthermore, one glance at our own life clearly demonstrates that the dark man isn't just an abstract idea or an artistic curiosity, but that he really does weave his way in and out of our life on a regular basis. In fact, dark man experiences are so common that every adult has (or *should* have) at least one dark man story to tell. But have you ever stopped to consider why this is? Or what on earth is going on here? Well, the intention of this book is to look at this mystery and to tease out the stories and experiences into one coherent whole. We are going to unravel the dark man phenomenon.

Now, my own interest in the dark man began many years ago when I was little more than a baby. I suppose it may have had something to do with the fact that I have always had a tendency to recognise the *patterns* which exist within things. And, as an adult, this tendency probably explains why I have been drawn towards philosophy, which looks at patterns of argument or reason, and linguistics, which is concerned with patterns of language. However, way back when I was small, the patterns that caught my eye were the ones I saw within the world around me and, a little later on, in people's words and behaviour. And it didn't take me long to recognise the dark man at work within all these things.

Then, leaping forward a number of years to when I was in my late twenties and early thirties, I had two particularly powerful dark man experiences. The first of these had me variously fearing for my life and doubting my sanity – fortunately both remained solidly intact – while the second occurred when I 'woke up' while under general anaesthetic. A consequence of these encounters was that I began to look for answers about what was going on here! I wanted an explanation! However, the more I searched, the more I realised that my experiences, although intense, were not unique. And I also began to appreciate just how many people have real, significant and sometimes tragic difficulties with the dark man.

So although I eventually found my answers, I was then faced with a dilemma about what to do with the information. Initially, my plan had been to develop the ideas so I could use them in my own studies. However, the more I looked around me, the more this seemed a pretty self-centred thing to do. Therefore I changed direction and began to write *The Dark Man* in the hope that it might help open people's eyes to the bigger picture of which we are all a part, and maybe ease their hearts a little with respect to the dark man – for, believe me, over the years a *hell* of a lot of guff has been spoken about this old entity, and goodness knows how much suffering has been induced or inflicted in his name.

How you approach the book, though, is wholly up to you. It has been written so you can read it from cover to cover as an unfolding story, or, alternatively, you may want to use it as a type of guide book – a traveller's guide – with headings and subheadings to help you find what you need and orientate you as you proceed. *The Dark Man* is divided into four parts:

- chapters 1 and 2 look at things from a fairly abstract point of view, in that we think about who (or what) the dark man may be and the different forms he can take;
- in chapters 3 and 4, we widen our perspective to consider the environment in which the dark man is found and the function he has within that environment;
- in chapters 5 and 6, we step back even further to examine the dark man from the wider perspective of our own lives, and to consider our relationship with him and some of the ways people react towards him;
- in the conclusion, we sum up why *knowing* the dark man and *walking with* him really do matter, before considering what the ultimate outcome of these experiences may actually be.

However, before we begin this journey there are several things I would like to make very clear. First, the dark man and the dark man phenomenon are in no way symbolic of, or connected to, any particular group of people. Indeed, the dark man phenomenon crosses time, borders, gender, colour, creed, age and class. In my work, first as a nurse and then as a teacher, I have had the pleasure of working with people from goodness knows how many different nationalities and faiths from every corner of the planet. I have listened as they have shared their stories, experiences and insights about all manner of things. And, without doubt, I can say that although people from different backgrounds do tend to interpret certain things in specific ways (as we shall soon see), one common thread that weaves its way through so very many of their tales is the usually unpleasant and/or frightening dark man.

Second, I would like to point out that although the dark man is often associated with spiritual and religious ideologies and practices, this book *in no way* takes a spiritualised stance towards him. Instead, all I am aiming to do is present an objective and accessible study of the phenomenon, which I hope you will find inherently interesting and which may reveal a somewhat deeper layer to life and being than you may be accustomed to looking at.

Third, I would like to stress that as the dark man is a naturally occurring phenomenon you do *not* need to be a super-enlightened being, or obtain the help of guides, gurus, spiritual instructors or paraphernalia of any kind to experience him. Yet, on the other hand, I must add that while the dark man is a naturally occurring phenomenon which the vast majority of us can simply observe unfolding around ourselves with no difficulty whatsoever, he can also be an extremely powerful occurrence that can (and does) cause some people considerable distress. Usually, though, just understanding the process is enough to resolve any issues we may have, and the book should be of help here. However, sometimes, and for some people, this

4

will not be enough. Therefore if you ever feel that things are 'getting out of hand' with the dark man, *please* seek professional help as soon as possible.

Finally, please don't *ever* try to 'induce' or 'intensify' these experiences through the use of mind-altering substances and/or practices. Yes, I know that some people do this without apparent side-effect or harm. But I also know that in susceptible individuals these behaviours can 'let loose a flood of sufferings of which no sane person ever dreamed'.[1] Furthermore, as I have already mentioned, such practices and trappings *aren't even necessary*, as all any of us have to do to see these things is open our eyes, open our heart and approach them with the consideration and respect they deserve. So, with all this said, let us now begin...

Chapter 1

The Dark Man

The dark man is ubiquitous. People from all times and all places have recorded their experiences of him in stories, poems, paintings, songs, stone, dance, crafts and prayers. Saint or sinner, scientist or theologian, agnostic or true believer, it makes little difference as the dark man has walked beside us since the very beginning and he will stay with us until the end. He is so intrinsic to the human experience that *everyone* has at least one dark man story to tell. And although many dark man experiences are pushed aside as we struggle on through life, many more are so extraordinarily significant that they cannot be dismissed and they often change the course of our life. Like it or not, the dark man is with us. He is real, valid and true. And he is not going away. So maybe the time has come to gather our resources and to turn to face the dark man, and when we do we might discover something very important about ourselves, our world and/or the universe in which we live.

The snag is, or rather *the snags are*, that, first, if the dark man was the sugar-plum man who lived on butter-kissed mountain we might be a tad more inclined to turn and look him in the eye. But unfortunately (or should this read 'thankfully'?) at no stretch of the imagination could this 'entity' ever be considered sweet. There is a lot of bunkum propagated about the dark man – some of which is simply due to misunderstanding, while a lot more can be considered deliberate misinformation – but the one thing that almost everyone does agree on is that the dark man is not the easiest 'person' to be around. Indeed, if the stories, poems, paintings, etc. are to be believed, the dark man is a loathsome, terrifying, implacable, disturbing force of nature. So, naturally enough, any sane person would be extremely reluctant to deliberately turn to meet him. Yet the problem is that the dark man is already here. We already have to live our lives with him stalking our every move. So maybe, now that we are grown-ups, the time has come to take a deep breath and to turn to face the 'monster'. And I'll tell you now: the dark man is not quite as atrocious as you may initially think; he is, in fact, one of the truest allies any of us will ever know.

The second snag which might prevent people from opening their eyes to the dark man is the view they have of the world. For instance, if you think that the world and everything in it is a neat collection of atoms, molecules and other solid stuff, then you may be reluctant to consider something which is, on the face of it, somewhat insubstantial. Similarly, for someone who adheres to a modern scientific view of the world, the dark man may seem too akin to mysticism or primitive superstition to warrant consideration. Now, I have absolutely no intention of undermining anyone's world view. But, then again, I don't have to, as empirical evidence clearly demonstrates that the dark man – whoever or whatever he may be – is a very real phenomenon and it is this phenomenon that I am interested in here. Admittedly, I shall shortly consider some possible explanations as to who or what the dark man may be. But, as you will see, he is equally understandable from the angles of science, psychology and spirit. So for this reason, I'll have to leave it for you to decide upon his true nature for yourselves.

Finally, one further snag that may get in the way of our meeting the dark man is language. Now, language is wonderful. It is varied, creative and meaningful. But it does have its limitations, as while language is particularly effective at describing, explaining and analysing material constructs, on the whole, it can't handle the less material side of experience. For example, think of something as complicated as an internal combustion engine or a particle accelerator. Language can effortlessly describe these things down to their most infinitesimal minutiae so that they can (in theory) be clearly and unambiguously understood by anyone. Now try to describe something as common and relatively 'simple' as love or happiness or even the colour blue. It is impossible to do, as such things defy rational explanation. Therefore when we want to express our knowledge and insights about immaterial events we find ourselves having to resort to metaphor, symbol and other creative devices, which although understandable are more open to personal interpretation and so cannot be regarded as unambiguously clear.

Now this is a problem for the dark man, as although he is certainly a part of our everyday world, it would be a mistake to think of him as a solid structure which occupies a space within it. Thus language can find itself staggering and straining whenever we try to explicitly describe him, or our experiences of him, to anyone else. What's more, although the language that is used to describe the dark man is often concise, creative and subtle, there are many people out there who simply choose to ignore, condemn or deride *anything* that cannot be explained in rational linear terms, reduced to a physical equation or replicated in a laboratory. And this is unfortunate, as these are often the same people that could do a great deal to further our understanding of the 'wider world' of which the dark man is a part, instead of simply leaving it to the theologians, mystics, artists and more metaphysically minded philosophers to explain. Now I am certainly *not* saying that science can take the place of any of these disciplines. It's just that a more analytical approach may possibly help to further our understanding of a phenomenon that is unarguably real, extremely significant and at times bewilderingly intense.

So, this said, let us now turn our attention back to the dark man as we begin to unravel the riddle of who (or what) he might be. And we shall do this by first considering what constitutes a *typical* dark man experience.

A Typical Dark Man Experience

As I have said, the dark man is both intrinsic and universal. That is, he has appeared to men and women throughout time, whatever culture they may belong to, whatever their place in society, and regardless of whatever god they may (or may not) have worshipped. It is possible to look at a text that has been written, drawn, carved, crafted or passed down in oral tradition from a Siberian shaman, an ancient Egyptian priest, a classical poet, a religious disciple, a native visionary and so on, and immediately recognise the dark shadow that passes through it as the same dark figure that stalks us through our own dreams today. Admittedly, there are variations in how individual people interpret what they experience. But then again, we can only ever see with the eyes of our time and I shall come to the subject 'colouring' shortly. Yet rub away the cultural overlay and it soon becomes apparent that human beings have been living and reliving the same dark man experience throughout history.

This does not mean, though, that the dark man experience is like a digital recording which is identical in all respects every time anyone sees or hears it. Instead, it seems to have more in common with something like *a greeting*, the niceties of which may differ between particular instances (for example, we may say 'hello', shake hands or kiss), while the basic format always remains the same. Similarly, while the particulars of a dark man experience can vary (for instance, sometimes he might take the form of a ominous presence while at other times we may see him as a dark-clothed man), beneath these differences there is a typical pattern of characteristics that is representative of very many, if not most, dark man encounters.

Generally speaking, a dark man experience begins when a **dark character** suddenly appears in our dreams, in the hypnogogic state between waking and sleeping, in our reverie, in our daydreams or before our fully awake conscious mind. The darkness might be an aspect of his appearance, such as his skin tone ('swarthy' is a term that is often used to describe him) and/or his clothing, or, perhaps more tellingly, the aura or atmosphere which surrounds him. He (for this character is *always* recognisable as **male** even when there are no obvious signs of gender), is usually described as **disturbing, chilling** or **frightening**. And although he usually appears at **night**, especially midnight or three o'clock in the morning, in actuality he can appear at any time and it may simply be that we are less distracted by other things in the hours of darkness. It does seem, though, that the guise the dark man takes varies according to the perceptions, expectations and experiences of the individuals concerned; but a **predatory assailant**, such as an intruder, stalker, attacker, murderer, incubus, vampiric seducer or lady killer, is common, as is the **Devil, Death** or **'filth'**. The dark man is also said to take the form of, or be accompanied by, a **large dark animal**, typically a dog or a wolf. And he is almost always **silent**, seldom speaking, at least in words. So, taken together, these elements amount to what we might call a 'classic' dark man experience. But it is also possible to experience just one or two of them in isolation. Indeed, very often the only sign of the dark man that we have is a **shadowy, dark (often ominous) presence** that we sense somewhere around us or that we catch slipping from our peripheral view as we turn our heads or enter a room.

Now, as I have said, the dark man phenomenon is ubiquitous. That is, there is no getting away from it. And sooner or later we all find ourselves, usually to our absolute horror, butted up against him. Furthermore, meeting the dark man can be a disturbing or frightening experience, particularly as we know so little about him, and especially since the little that we do know has probably been gleaned from the guff which has been promulgated about him for so long. Anyhow, dark man experiences tend to be a tad unnerving and consequently, when we do meet him, we typically react by dropping into one of several defence mechanisms – the most common of which is to run, fast, in the opposite direction – or by drawing on superstition, folk magic and other protective devices – such as sleeping with the light on – in an attempt to ward off the dark stranger. Unfortunately though, these are not particularly useful responses as they both work and don't work at the same time. But we'll come back to this paradox later.

Yet not everyone reacts to the dark man in this way, and throughout history many brave and curious souls have quelled their anxieties and turned to examine their own and other people's experiences in an attempt to understand what might be going on. They might have been alerted to the significance of the phenomenon by the fact that dark man experiences are often powerful life-changing occurrences; or possibly by the consideration that something so widespread must have an underlying significance; then again, they may simply have wanted to understand the dark man so they could help others deal with the experience. I don't know. But we shall now take a look at the explanations that several of these people have given us before we continue our own journey to understand the dark man.

Storytellers, Mythographers, Poets and Psychologists: Explaining the Dark Man

Storytellers

Story is a traditional medium whereby people make sense of their world by conceptualising and containing their experiences within a familiar and understandable setting. Whether as a myth, a crafted piece of literature, a popular novel, a folk or fairytale, a motion picture, a TV soap opera, a personal fantasy, or even, in some senses, a dream, stories allow us to understand and explore everything from lofty concepts such as God to more down-to-earth issues such as the dangers which await young girls who walk alone in the forest. Through the words and imagery of their stories, the storytellers relate their observations and insights about the world in which we live. And, from the very beginning, their stories have included the character of the dark man.

They don't always call him 'the dark man', of course. But despite this, he is one of the most easily recognisable elements in any tale. In his most basic guise he can appear as the 'bogeyman': the primal fear who lurks in the darkest corners and who can be held at bay by warm blankets wrapped snugly around us, by lighting a fire or by turning on a light. He never truly goes away of course, but the old prophylactic magic does create a safe enough space to allow small children, and their parents, to sleep soundly at night.

Yet in other stories the dark man acquires a more 'solid' form, such as the big bad wolf, the black knight, the dark lord, the unwholesome stranger, the predatory assailant or the diabolical beast. We shall be looking at these characterisations in more detail in chapter 2 and again in chapter 6, but for now it's enough to say that when the dark man appears in these guises the story-teller is telling us that change, or disruption to the status quo, is either imminent or long overdue. What's more, the old magic isn't much use here. Imagine Frodo Baggins trying to save Middle Earth with a fluffy blanket. No, the storytellers understand that when the dark man has gathered enough energy to project himself forward as a 'man' or a 'monster', all we can do is gather our resources for the changes and challenges which lie ahead.

So, as you can see, storytellers don't tend to analyse and argue that the dark man is this or that. It isn't their 'job' to do so. Instead they delve into the phenomenon, demonstrating how the dark man interacts with the world, and exploring the different ways in which we might deal with him. So, in this sense, story moves from being mere entertainment to become something that reveals and examines profound truths about, or the underlying dynamics of, the world. Thereby story is less of a theory into the nature of the dark man so much as a 'survival guide' for coping with him. And both Joseph Campbell and Clarissa Pinkola Estés use stories in this way.

Joseph Campbell

In his classic book *The Hero with a Thousand Faces*, Joseph Campbell introduces us to the idea of the 'monomyth'. That is, the single common story upon which all other myths, folktales, and even our own dreams are built, and which offers us insight into 'the riddle of life'. He argues that the monomyth is a fundamental structure within which archetypal characters play out their allotted roles in various guises, time and time again in an eternal round, and that the same structure underlies our own lives. Consequently, the old tales – especially the hero narrative, within which an ordinary person takes up a challenge or disappears on a quest, faces many obstacles, trials and occult forces, before returning home a changed person cradling a gift from the gods – take on a deeper significance in that they become way-markers, maps or 'guides' for our own life.

In his book, Campbell identifies and explores a number of archetypal elements which he believes are inherent within this story of life. And in his description of the character he calls the 'herald'[1] we can clearly see reflections of the dark man. The herald, he says, is 'often dark, loathy, or terrifying, judged evil by the world'; appears when our old way of life no longer serves us; and can take various forms, such as a beast, a black knight, or a 'mysterious veiled figure'. Moreover, although we may not consciously recognise or particularly like this character, on an unconscious level the herald can be 'profoundly familiar', and once it makes itself known, 'what was formally meaningful may become strangely emptied of value'. We shall look at how the dark man is closely connected to our values, needs and desires, later in the book. But for now it's worth noting that, as Campbell understands it, although the herald may seem unattractive or unpleasant, if we just follow him, 'the way would be opened through the walls of day into the dark where the jewels glow'. In other words, the herald [dark man] opens the way to that which is truly valuable in our lives.

Robert Graves

Robert Graves also recognises an underlying story or 'Theme' to life which is populated by certain figures. But as a poet he is less concerned with explaining this as an abstraction, as he is about living his life and expressing himself in a way that is true to it. The Theme, he says in his book *The White Goddess*, underlies all true poetry and while appreciation of it was once everywhere, it is now only implicit in the 'celebration of the festivals now known as Candlemas, Lady Day, May Day, Midsummer Day, Lammas, Michaelmas, All-Hallowe'en' and Christmas', and it was also 'secretly preserved as religious doctrine in the covens of the anti-Christian witch-cult'.[2]

According to Graves, the Theme revolves around the story of the birth, life, death and resurrection of the God of the Waxing Year (whose role the poet adopts), the Triple Goddess (embodied by the poet's muse), and the God of the Waning Year (who is seen as the poet's rival, blood-brother, or weird). Furthermore, Graves observes that these three characters are such a fundamental part of our 'racial inheritance' that they 'not only assert themselves in poetry but recur on occasions of emotional stress in the form of dreams, paranoiac visions and delusions'.[3]

The White Goddess is a remarkable book, but it is also, by Graves' own admission, a 'difficult' one.[4] Yet, for our purposes, it is sufficient to note that the character Graves knows as 'the King of the Waning Year', or the 'rival', appears to be yet another embodiment of the dark man. As he says:

> The weird, or rival, often appears in nightmare as the tall, lean, dark-faced bed-side spectre, or Prince of the Air, who tries to drag the dreamer out through the window, so that he

looks back and sees his body still lying rigid in bed; but he takes countless other malevolent or diabolic or serpent-like forms.[5]

As you can tell, Graves had little love for the rival [dark man], but he did understand him to be an *essential* element in the eternal and fundamental round he knew as the Theme. Moreover, when I first read *The White Goddess*, and for that matter *The Hero with a Thousand Faces*, I was struck by the fact that my own experiences were sometimes directly opposite, 180 degrees opposed, to those described by both Graves and Campbell. In a way, though, this isn't too surprising as the idea that the feminine has a different type of relationship with the dark man is fundamental to Graves' understanding of the Theme, and Campbell also notes that men's and women's experience of the monomyth differs in places.[6] However, this is not to say that women necessarily find the dark man pleasant or likeable, as this is simply not the case, and these two books, as well as our own examination of the dark man, continue to be relevant to all.

Clarissa Pinkola Estés
In her book *Women Who Run with the Wolves*, the Jungian analyst and storyteller Clarissa Pinkola Estés explains that 'In a single human being there are many other beings, all with their own values, motives and devices'[7] and through her analysis of women's dreams and the story *Bluebeard* she discusses the psychological entity of the dark man.

The dark man, she says, is an intense and potentially ruthless aspect of the psyche, which turns up time and time again in creative works, such as poetry, myth and fairytale, and also in our dreams. Indeed, Dr Estés claims that dark man dreams are 'so common it is remarkable if a woman has reached age twenty-five without having had [one]'.[8] And she also observes that dark man dreams have an initiatory quality in that they act as wake-up calls telling us that something is amiss in our life; that we are about to make a shift from one level of being and knowing to another higher level; or as warnings that if we don't attend to the things we hold dear then they will be lost. As she says:

> The threat of the dark man serves as a warning to all of us – if you don't pay attention to your treasures they will be stolen from you. In this manner, when a woman has one or a series of these dreams, it means that a huge gate is opening to the initiatory grounds where her revaluing of her gifts can occur. There, whatever has been incrementally destroying her or robbing her can be recognised, apprehended and dealt with.[9]

So, overall, there seems to be a general consensus that the dark man appears in our lives when a time of change is either at hand or possibly long overdue. However, on the surface at least, there looks to be much less agreement about who (or what) he actually is: Clarissa Pinkola Estés understands him to be an archetype, though as we shall see this is not quite as straightforward a concept as it may seem; to Robert Graves he is an old god; and Joseph Campbell takes the view that the 'herald' is one element of a cosmogenic round upon which metaphysics, psychology and myth all rest. As for me, I have to admit that, *logically speaking*, I think it is very difficult, if not impossible, to determine the precise nature of the dark man, so in this respect I take an agnostic-type stance towards him. However, on a more *emotional level*, I accept it can be equally difficult living with such an open-ended attitude, as human beings seem to *need* a model of reality on which to hang their experiences. So for this reason, we shall now examine several different ways of understanding who (or what) the dark man may be.

Models of Understanding

The Dark Man as an Old God

All ancient cultures worshipped their own pantheons, or families, of gods and, taken together, these animal-headed, toga-wearing, hammer-wielding deities appear, on the surface at least, a pretty disparate bunch. However, what our ancestors did agree on was that the old gods were *living, thinking, feeling, autonomous beings* and that although they lived in their own world (be it called Heaven, Olympus, the Underworld, etc.) they would also spend time in our world where they would meet and mingle, advise and assist, and otherwise interact with human beings. These gods were also held to have been responsible for the act of creation, or at least for the creation of human beings, and they were often credited with maintaining the balance of all things. However, old gods also tended to be very fallible deities in that they would, if the whim came upon them, use human beings as their 'playthings', engineering encounters and challenges to test us and to toy with our emotions, and they were notoriously susceptible to the baser human sentiments, such as lust, jealousy, rage and revenge.

Now, following this model of understanding, I have *absolutely no doubt* that the dark inexorable god, who appears time and time again in different cultural contexts, is exactly the same entity that we today know as 'the dark man'. Our ancestors knew him by different names, of course, and described him using the language of their time. But whether he appears as *Set, Hades, Pluto, Lucifer,* etc. this dark chthonian entity was generally acknowledged to be one of the most complicated, challenging and downright fright-ening of all the gods, and, what's more, he continues to be a challenging part of our own lives today.

Nevertheless, it must be pointed out that there is a world of difference between saying that the dark man phenomenon lies behind our ancestors' experiences and saying that the dark man is a 'living, thinking, feeling, autonomous being', and especially that he is a being who is subject to emotions such as love, rage or jealousy. We shall return to the problem of whether the dark man may, or may not, be a conscious entity when we look at *The Dark Man as a Law of Nature*. However, for now, it is enough to say that, as I understand it, this problem is the one reason why we may never understand what the dark man really is and that ultimately any answer must rest on your own beliefs. In other words, if you believe that the dark man is a sapient and/or sentient being, then, to all intents, you hold that he is an old god, while if you can't accept that this entity has independent consciousness, then you'll have to look for your answers elsewhere.

The Dark Man as a Law of Nature
Laws of Nature are blind dynamics. That is, they have no foresight, no hindsight, no compassion, no understanding, no soul; in fact they have no conscious element whatsoever. They simply do what they do – end of story. Gravity is an example of a law of nature: we can't see it, taste it, touch it, etc. but we know that it is there because every time we throw a ball into the air the same ball always falls back to the ground. Similarly, laws of nature govern the way flowers grow, our bodies age, the weather changes, the seasons pass and the heavens roll. In fact, any time we see a *regular pattern* occurring in the natural world we can be sure that it is underpinned by a law of nature.

Laws of nature can be more or less 'homely', in that they may affect very localised things, such as the way our pupils contract in bright sunlight, or they might be wider in their application, such as those that govern the formation of a galaxy. However, if we push our imagination right out to the beginning of every-thing, to around the time of the Big Bang, we're told that the universe itself was formed by a just a handful of these laws. That is, *a small number of fundamental laws of nature created and maintain everything that we know*, which very obviously includes us, our bodies, our minds,[10] our surroundings, the natural environment, the seasons, the skies, and so on. It also means that the effects of these fundamental laws can be observed as *universal patterns* within all these things today.

Therefore, following this model, it is quite easy to see that the character we are referring to as 'the dark man' may be a person-ification of one of these fundamental laws: he has been with us, in our minds and bodies, from the very beginning; he is found within our relationships, societies and our cultures; and he is inherent within all of nature. Indeed, it is quite possible that the regular patterns we experience in our dreams, in nature, and which are depicted within the mythological round are 'simply' the effects of this impersonal, fundamental dynamic. Thus, if I were a brilliant scientist, I might be able to reduce the dark man to a mathematical equation, whereupon he might be known as *Wells' Law of Conversion*, or some such thing. But as I'm not a scientist (brilliant or otherwise) this isn't going to happen, so I am afraid we'll just have to continue working with the everyday concept of 'the dark man'.

Now as I said, it is very much a matter of *belief* whether we take the dark man to be a conscious being, or whether we think he is a blind dynamic which is devoid of consciousness, thought and feeling, and that any *apparent signs* of consciousness he may display are nothing more than our own tendency to *project our own personality* onto inanimate objects, which we then mistakenly take to be autonomous, sentient, sapient things. It is an old stalemate, whereby the spiritual and the material are seen as conflicting explanations of all that is; and one which those who argue in favour of God's existence and those who claim that there is no God have been wrangling about for centuries. However, leaving God, who is way beyond the scope of this book, aside, there may be a third way of explaining who (or what) the dark man is, which, on the surface at least, does seem to sidestep the spiritual versus material dilemma. It is the position taken by

Clarissa Pinkola Estés, Robert Graves and very many others. It is the idea that the dark man is a universal archetype.

The Dark Man as an Archetype

Today the term 'archetype' is more or less restricted to the way the psychologist Carl Gustav Jung used it in his psychological theories. According to Jung, archetypes are fundamental predispositions or 'organs' of the mind. They are inherent or inborn within all of us. And taken together they make up the deep layer of the unconscious mind that Jung referred to as the *collective unconscious*. To begin with, archetypes have no particular form, that is, they are 'empty', and they only become visible to us when they 'pick up' specific images from a person's life. Moreover, as they are predominantly visual in nature, archetypes tend to work as products of the imagination, whereby they regularly appear as characters in our dreams, neuroses, fantasies, mythologies, religious iconographies, fairytales, etc.[11]

It is important to realise, however, that archetypes are not mere psychological novelties, but that they actually work to organise, reformulate and filter the dizzying kaleidoscope of information that our senses are bombarded with at any moment. So, in this respect, archetypes are the necessary lenses through which we see ourselves, our world, and through which we interpret our entire reality. As Jung noted, this makes them analogous with Plato's forms (*eidola*) and Kant's categories of reason.[12] And it means that archetypes aren't simply inert or passive aspects of the psyche but that they actively and dynamically work to shape our thoughts and experiences. As Jung put it:

[Just] as the organs of the body are not mere lumps of indifferent, passive matter, but are dynamic, functional complexes which assert themselves with imperious urgency, so also the archetypes, as organs of the psyche, are dynamic instinctual complexes which determine psychic life to an extraordinary degree. That is why I also call them *dominants* of the unconscious.[13]

Therefore archetypes shape and interpret our experiences, and by so doing they determine the way we think, feel and act. So, in this respect, it is easy to see that archetypes are hugely powerful psychological complexes, which affect not only the individual person, but also the many individual people who share similar life experiences and who comprise a family, a society, a country or a culture. So archetypes really do shape our world!

Moreover, following this model, it is easy to understand how the dark man can be universal and ubiquitous; how he can significantly affect our lives; and how he can appear as the dark stranger, black knight, big bad wolf, predator, animal groom, Lord of the Underworld, Death, and so on. It also explains how a small child who hasn't yet acquired the life experiences to 'colour', or give form to, this particular psychological complex might see him as the faceless dark bogeyman.

Now, while I am *extremely attracted* to the idea that the dark man is a universal archetype, I have to admit that there are a couple of problems with this model of understanding. The first, and perhaps the most obvious, is that as Jung's theory of archetypes is a *psychological* theory it can only explain *psychological* occurrences; but as you will see, the dark man phenomenon is certainly not limited to the human mind. Admittedly, we *interpret* our dark man experiences via our psyche, but on the other hand the heavens roll, the seasons pass and life turns to death *whether we happen to be looking or not.*[14, 15]

Furthermore, there is a second, more significant, objection to the idea that the dark man is an archetype and it is that, from the perspective of explaining who (or what) the dark man may be, the whole archetype theory is something of a red herring, as it is a theory about *how the mind works* but not a theory about *what the mind is.* In other words, it suggests why we see the dark man the way we do, or why he affects us the way he does – and these are important things to know – but it tells us nothing about what the mind, and thereby what the dark man who is said to be a psychological complex, actually is.

Now as I said, the mind is a tricky issue. But for the sake of argument, we can cut through the confusion and separate all the conflicting theories into two basic camps: those who think that matter is the fundamental substance out of which everything (including mind) is made, and those who think that mind is the fundamental stuff of creation.[16] In modern philosophy these two opposing views are known as *materialism* and *idealism*, respectively. And Jung himself was aware of the tension between these two standpoints which he called the *Western view* and the *Eastern view* of the mind.[17]

Simply speaking, the materialist or traditional 'Western' view is that matter is the basic stuff of the universe. Everything is composed of it. Thereby everything we know is the product of the many different ways that matter can come together. We are made of matter. Our bodies are made of matter. Even our consciousness, our thoughts and our feelings are merely the products of our massively complex material brains. Jung noted that, following this view, the idea of *psychic heredity* (i.e. the inheritance of mental phenomena) can be understood in *a narrow sense* as the inheritance from our parents of certain *physical characteristics* (e.g. cell structure) which have an overall tendency to express themselves in particular psychological ways, for example as personality traits or as the universal predispositions of mind we know as *archetypes*.[18] So, following this, it is reasonable to assume that *if* the dark man is an archetype, and *if* an archetype is a product of our material brain, then the events that we know as 'the dark man phenomenon' could certainly be an outward expression of one of the fundamental *laws of nature* that we looked at earlier, which shape and maintain everything we know.

Yet on the other hand, idealism, or the traditional 'Eastern'

view of the mind, states that mind and not matter is the fundamental stuff of all things. Now there are two ways to take this.
First, it can mean that all the material stuff we see around us is,
at its most fundamental level, mind made solid or 'densified'
mind. And it is worth pointing out that this view isn't a million
miles away from what new physics is discovering about the
nature of the universe. Second, it can mean that we are all living
a type of dream, whereby everything we see around us is
nothing more than *maya* or illusion, and this particular view has
been taught in esoteric schools and conveyed by mystics,
metaphysicians and certain philosophers for thousands of years.

Actually, these two ways of thinking about mind do overlap
somewhat and they both invite a mass of knotty problems, such
as 'Whose mind is it anyway?', which I have absolutely *no*
intention of going into here. But one thing I shall say is that *if* the
dark man is one of the fundamental building blocks of mind that
Jung called an archetype, and *if* mind is the fundamental
substance of all things, then the dark man must be one of the
fundamental building blocks of all things. Moreover, *if* mind
comprises all things, then all things must be imbued with
mind/consciousness; therefore the dark man must be a conscious
co-creator of the universe. That is, he must be an *old god*.

So although the idea that the dark man is an archetype
explains why we see him the way we do and, to a greater or
lesser degree, why he has the effect on us and our lives that he
has, it cannot manage to bridge the spiritual versus material
dilemma that has divided so many people for so long – and
which will probably continue to divide us for a long time to
come. As Jung says in his psychological commentary to the
Eastern esoteric guide for the recently departed soul, *The Tibetan
Book of the Dead*:

The world of gods and spirits is truly 'nothing but' the
collective unconscious inside me. To turn this sentence round

so that it reads: The collective unconscious is the world of gods and spirits outside me, no intellectual acrobatics are needed, but a whole human lifetime, perhaps even many lifetimes of increasing completeness. Notice that I do not say 'of increasing perfection', because those who are 'perfect' make another kind of discovery altogether.[19]

So what we have seen in this chapter is that the dark man is a legitimate, significant, but also very challenging entity, who appears in our dreams, imagination, stories, myths, waking experiences, etc. and whom we must all meet at various points in our life. We have also seen that he typically appears at times of change, or when change is long overdue, but that there is much less agreement about who (or what) he actually is, and that people's opinions regarding his true nature tend to be shaped by their beliefs about the nature of the universe – that is, whether we live in a spiritual (i.e. conscious/intelligent) universe, or one that is composed wholly of inert matter – rather than by unassailable fact. I also suggested that this spiritual versus material dichotomy is very old and probably irreducible and that, consequently, it might be more prudent to take an agnostic-type stance towards the dark man instead of wasting time and energy trying to pigeon-hole something that is essentially unfathomable. However, I also suggested that such an 'open ended' approach might not suit everyone, as people often need to draw on models of understanding to help them make sense of their experiences and the world around them.

We then looked at three different ways of understanding who (or what) the dark man may be. First, we considered the more spiritual idea that he might be an *old god*. Then, we looked at the more material concept of a *law of nature*. And finally, we considered whether he might be a psychological complex or *archetype*. However, we also saw that there is a significant overlap between the old god and law of nature models and that both ultimately rest on our beliefs. And that although the idea of the dark man as an archetype does seem to answer many of the questions surrounding the phenomenon, it cannot bridge the spiritual versus material dilemma which exists between the traditional 'Eastern' and 'Western' concepts of reality and mind.

So with this said, I must now leave it to *you* to decide how *you* feel the dark man is best understood. But for the remainder of this book I shall be using the terms *old god, law of nature* and *archetype* (almost) interchangeably.

Chapter 2

Meeting the Dark Man

In the previous chapter we considered what *a typical dark man experience* involves and we saw that it generally begins when a frightening and/or disturbing dark character suddenly appears in our dreams, imagination or wakeful consciousness. This being is almost always perceived as male. And it can be interpreted by the individual in subtly different ways, e.g. as a dark shadow, an assailant, a predator or Death. In this chapter I would like to build on this basic outline to examine in more detail the different guises that the dark man can take, the things he tends to be associated with, and the places and times where we are most likely to meet him. And the reason I want to look at these areas is quite simply to help you recognise the dark man when you see him. You see, how the dark man appears depends on two things: (a) our previous life experiences: as with Jung's archetypes, we see him in ways that are familiar or which make sense to us, so while an ancient Egyptian might have seen the dark man as a jackal or a jackal-headed man, I may see him as a big bad wolf, an assailant or the tall, gaunt Reaper; and (b) the state of our relationship to him.

Now, we shall come back to the subject of our relationship to the dark man in later chapters. But for now, I shall just say that very often the *really frightening* and absolutely unmistakable dark man who shakes us to the core tends not to be the first dark man persona that we meet. It is not that he is ever delightful. But very often there are subtler indications of the dark man's presence long before he truly asserts himself. Admittedly, it is up to us whether we listen to these warning shots or not. But if we do, they at least give us the opportunity to act before the big guns truly rip into our lives. I would also like to emphasise that *not all dark man experiences are negative*. As I said, the dark man is one of the truest allies that any of us will ever know and very often valuable dark man experiences of reassurance, strength and support go unnoticed because most people don't have a clue what they are seeing, feeling, etc. So with this in mind, we shall now take a look at some of the more familiar forms the dark man can take.

What the Dark Man Looks Like

Human Form(s)
When the dark man appears in human form he is generally described as being a **tall, gaunt,** even **skeletal, swarthy-skinned** man, with **black hair, dark or black eyes** and **dark or black clothing**. He is often said to be **loathsome, disturbing, filthy, uncouth, unkempt, grotesque, marauding** or **diabolical**. Though, sometimes, he is described as **handsome** and **charming,** but this is often in a disturbing, frightening or **mesmeric** way. He also tends to be **silent**.

In this form the dark man has given substance to vampires, highwaymen and other gentlemen of the night. He has been depicted as a black knight or a fallen angel. And he is often interpreted in women's dreams as a murderer, prowler or intruder. I remember one dream in which I daren't go home because I didn't want the murderous dark stalker who was following me to know where I lived. So I journeyed for miles and miles to try and evade him, but no matter where I went or who I asked for help I couldn't escape. Likewise, another common dark man dream is where the marauder is actually *in the house*, and there is nowhere left to run, and he is getting closer and closer and closer. And Robert Graves' description of the 'tall, lean, dark-faced, bed-side spectre, or Prince of the Air'[1] is one more example of a personified dark man in our dreams.

Animal Form(s)

The dark man often appears in the form of an animal or as a man-animal hybrid and the animals he is most closely associated with are **horses, wolves, large dogs, bears, boars, bulls, donkeys, goats, 'beasts', monsters, serpents** and **frogs**. When embodying the dark man these animals are always **male**. They are frequently said to have **shaggy coats**. And they are almost always **black,** or some other **dark colour**, though **dull rust-red** is also common and **frogs can be green or pale gold**. Similarly, when the dark man appears as a man-animal hybrid he will adopt some of the animal's characteristics, such as the animal's head, its teeth, its shaggy coat, its hooves or claws, its tail, its cold clammy skin or its mannerisms. However, while these features can be very obvious, as with the bull-headed minotaur, they can also be more subtle, such as the vampire's elongated canines or Bluebeard's indigo-black facial hair.

The dark man in animal form is regularly found in folklore, myth, legend, fairytales and our dreams, where he may appear as a dragon with a taste for hapless virgins, a centaur, a big bad wolf, a ravenous werewolf or a small green frog who obligingly returns the little princess's golden ball. Interestingly, many of these tales centre on a female character who either establishes a close relationship with the dark creature (as do the two sisters in *Snow White and Rose Red*) or who sets up home with him (as does Belle in *Beauty and the Beast*). However, in stories with a male protagonist, the hero usually sets out to fight, capture or kill the creature, 'to rid the land of its deadly scourge', or some such thing. And what we are seeing here is an outplaying of Robert Graves' *Theme*, within which the male protagonist always loses the hand of his Lady to the dark diabolical Rival. In other words, we are being given a glimpse into how the masculine and the feminine relate differently to this ancient archetype.

Unstructured Form(s)

As we have seen, the dark man does not always take a physically perceptible form. The terrifying shadow or presence we call the **bogeyman** is one example of him appearing in a formless guise. And although this particular character is more usually associated with the hours of darkness and small children's bedrooms, the bogeyman can also appear to adults and in the light of day.

Of course, adults do not tend to use the term 'bogeyman' (which, incidentally, means 'hobgoblin') to describe the dark, disturbing presence they see or feel around them. Instead, they use expressions like **an atmosphere of darkness, an aura of fear** or **a feeling of imminent danger.** Also, the experience of a **shadow** or **presence** which appears at the edge of our visual field and which moves away or simply disappears whenever we try to look directly at it is very common. Moreover, people claim that these experiences are often accompanied by sensations of being **weighed down,** or of **apprehension, fear** or an **all-pervasive dread.** And it is said that feelings such as these can hang over physical locations, such as accident black-spots, or even over communities, towns or entire nations.

In his book *Hug the Monster,* the adventurer David Miln Smith recounts how, as part of a series of global challenges, he found himself locked up and alone for the night in St Michael's Cave on Gibraltar, and how, while he was there, he found himself experiencing the 'monster' that we are here calling the 'unstructured' dark man. He writes:

> Exhausted from transatlantic jet lag and a strenuous run through hilly Gibraltar carrying a symbolic torch earlier that day, I settled into my sleeping bag in a small chamber inside the cave. The cave came alive with unfamiliar noises as stalactites dripped and splattered on the sand and rock. My weary body left me with no mental defences for the terror that began

welling up as I tried to interpret the disconcerting, eerie sounds coming from below me somewhere in the pitch black tomb. Could those really be apes I hear? I panicked, grabbing for my flashlight, remembering stories of other explorers who'd vanished in the bottomless cave. The flashlight was no comfort, as its beam intercepted and transformed stalactites into a tribe of evil, disfigured, grinning faces that taunted me. My mind raced with fear, my breathing became shallow, and my body turned to rock. I thought my hair was turning white from the terror. I wished I had accepted the key so I could get out of that place. Unsure and disorientated, I was completely unable to move. Logic and objectivity only reinforced the horrifying facts: rock apes, lost explorers, bottomless cave. I was three years old again, facing the fierce, unrelenting monsters of my childhood imagination.[2]

And could Napoleon Bonaparte have experienced something similar when he spent the night in the King's Chamber of the Great Pyramid? No one knows for sure what happened while he was alone in the darkness, for he never said. But what is known is that the great general was ashen-faced and shaking when he emerged, and that he wished for the incident never to be spoken of again. Admittedly, over the years many suggestions have been made as to what might have taken place that night. But it is quite probable that what did happen was that, like David Miln Smith, Napoleon found himself in the company – in one form or another – of the formidable dark man.

What the Dark Man is Associated With

According to stories, myths and legends, all the old gods were associated with different times, places, acquaintances and bits and bobs of paraphernalia. Thus Aphrodite was associated with the morning and the evening, Artemis with untamed woodland, Demeter with the horse and Zeus with thunderbolts. Likewise, the dark man, who throughout history has been known by many names, is also associated with a number of specific objects, which again and again, and in different times and different places, appear alongside him.

In fact, we have already looked at a number of these associations, such as the colour black, fear, maleness, horses, wolves, etc. in the context of them *embodying* the dark man. However, it's important to realise that these things can also appear *alongside or around* him and in this respect they serve several purposes. First, they help us identify the dark man. So in a dream or story, if a character appears, and if this character is tall, dark and male, and if he arrives at night and in the company of black horses, wolves and so on, then we can be pretty certain that we are meeting the dark man. Second, although these associations may, on the face of it, look like a random list of symbols, this is certainly not the case, as they actually comprise a sophisticated commentary that we can use to help orientate ourselves in the darkness. We touched on this subject earlier and we shall return to it in more detail throughout the book. But for now, it is safe to say that many messages of insight, direction and reassurance are communicated by way of these associated symbols, but first we need to recognise what we are looking at. And third, many of these associations act as portals through which we can meet the dark man and/or assess the state of our relationship with him. This is an idea we shall return to shortly, but first we should take a look at some of the things that are commonly associated with the dark man.

Clothing and Accessories
In ancient Greek mythology Hades, the dark god of the Underworld whose name means 'the invisible' or 'sightless', possessed a **helmet of invisibility** that allowed him to walk unnoticed through our world, where he would keep himself informed of the deeds of his future subjects or fall lustily in love

with various beautiful maids. The idea of invisibility also crosses into the **black clothes** that the dark man is said to wear, which allow him to blend into the night or melt into the shadows. Similarly, the **mask** is another instance of this symbol. For example, the highwayman's mask enabled this semi-mythological 'gentleman of the road' to remain hidden or concealed from view as he went about his business of stealing gentlemen's treasures and ladies' hearts while mounted on his dark horse in the dead of night. Finally, the idea of invisibility has connotations of omnipresence, as we can never really be sure when the dark Lord of the Underworld will be standing behind us tallying our deeds and misdeeds, or when a gentleman of the night may emerge from the shadows and demand that we 'stand and deliver'. Therefore the wise among us would have to assume that this is happening, or that it is about to happen, right *now*.

The dark man is also closely associated with the idea of the *axis* which tends to reveal itself in his clothing and accessories as a **staff** or a **stick**, such as the punting stick used by Charon to ferry the dead across the river Styx, or perhaps most infamously as the **scythe**. However, that other male axial symbol, the sword, is seldom adopted by the dark man as the sword tends to penetrate into the earth as opposed to emerging from it. However, if the dark man were to carry such a weapon the chances are that it would be blue-black in colour and devastatingly sharp, or else black, rusty and dull.

The dark man is also said to own all the mineral wealth found beneath the surface of the earth. Thus he is closely connected to **jewels** and **precious ores**; with **gold** (and sometimes **silver**) being his metal of choice. However, the dark man's gold is usually pale yellow in colour, as opposed to the orange gold of solar symbolism, though when it is wrought into **rings, chains,** or even Hades' **golden chariot**, pale chthonian gold is often said to contain a fiery depth.

Associates

In myths and stories the dark man is often depicted as a loner, an outsider or a **stranger** in our world. This is not to say that he forms no associations, as he is closely allied to the female inhabitants of the Underworld, such as the **Fates** and **Hecate**. And as an extension of his relationship with these wise old women of the night, he is infamously associated with **witches**. Moreover, the dark man is connected to **women** in general. In fact, to sever the connection between a woman and the dark man (even at his most abhorrent) would be to cleave her soul in two: a fatal mutilation, but one that many have tried. As for men, well they too should think carefully before trying to rid themselves of the darkness, for although their relationship with the dark man is often, on the face of it, quite different from the relationship he tends to have with women, both the *masculine* and the *feminine* are inherent within us all. But more of this later.

Additionally, as we have already seen, the dark man is closely allied with a number of animals including **horses, wolves, dogs, bears, boars, bulls, donkeys, goats, 'beasts', monsters, serpents** and **frogs**; and when these animals appear in association with the dark man they are almost always **black or dark** in colour, are always **male** and are often said to have **shaggy coats**. As we have also seen, the dark man can adopt the form of any of these animals – a concept which is closely tied to the notion of the witch's familiar – or they can appear alongside him. But either way, the appearance of the animal will tend to have particular significance, in that, say, a bull will most likely appear at a different point on 'the path' from either a donkey or a serpent.

Yet some caution is required when interpreting these symbols as, like all archetypes, they are coloured by our actual life experiences. Thus, in my own dreams, *horses, wolves/dogs* and *bulls* overwhelmingly predominate and other clues have to be discerned from their colours, attitudes, behaviour, the environment, etc.

Environment

Roughly speaking, the environment can be divided into features that are naturally occurring and those which are man-made. In relation to the natural environment, the dark man is fundamentally associated with the qualities of **darkness, earth** and **death.** Thus we find him in proximity to that which is **underground,** such as the earth's **mineral wealth** or the **Underworld,** and to deep dark **caves, forests** or **pools of water.** The dark man is also associated with the idea of the **material world,** or **matter** *per se,* and also with **filth, excrement** and **decay,** which combines the qualities of earth or matter and death. He is also connected to **natural barriers** or **boundaries,** such as **high cliffs, rivers** or the **tree-line,** and to **barren, rocky or volcanic landscapes.** Finally, as we have seen, the dark man is also associated with the idea of the **axis,** which in the natural environment often appears as a **single tree,** a **tall tree,** a **tall tree with deep roots** or a **single branch.**

Man-made **barriers, boundaries** and **limits** are also connected to the dark man, but in this case they take the form of a **wall,** a **moat** or some other artefact. The dark man is also associated with the way over or through these obstacles. Thus we may see him in association with a **gateway,** a **doorway** or a **bridge.** Indeed, throughout history the dark man has regularly been depicted in the role of gatekeeper, door-warden, bridge-master or ferryman. He is also associated with **paths** and **roads,** especially **crossroads** and **forks in the road, dark paths** and **alleyways,** and **underground passageways** and **tunnels. Hidden rooms,** and to a lesser extent **secret gardens,** are also connected to the dark man, as are the **keys** or **riddles** that are often required to access or escape these places.

Times

The times most closely associated with the dark man are the **winter solstice** and the hour of **midnight,** and the **summer solstice** and the hour of **midday.** Moreover, these four times have long been regarded as hugely portentous junctures in that they have been seen as the *hinges* or *pivots* on which life and time turn, or as the *doorways* through which all things must pass if the *cycles of life* are to continue.

The winter solstice occurs on the shortest day and the longest night. It is the coldest, darkest time of year when the earth is most bereft of the sun's light and warmth. And it is the doorway through which all things must pass if light and life are to return to the world. Similarly, midnight is the hinge on which one day swings to the next.[3] And both midnight and the winter solstice have traditionally been regarded as ominous times, for when the doorways swing open, the natural barrier between darkness/death and light/life is removed; the dead are able to walk abroad; and the terrible, gaunt Lord of the Underworld strides out into the world of man.

On the other hand, the summer solstice and midday are times of life and light, when the sun is at its zenith and when shadows are banished from the earth... apparently – for even in the light and warmth of the sun it should not be forgotten that the summer solstice and midday are also turning points on which the doorway between light/life and darkness/death swings open. It is just that at these times when the Lord of the Underworld steps out into the world of the living, he is rendered invisible by the glare of the sun – in the same way that the sunny skies of day conceal the indigo of the midnight sky. Thus he takes on the *mantle of invisibility* that Hades did when he donned his magical helmet.

Finally, it is also important to note that *the cycles of life* are not confined to the yearly and daily cycles, but that our own lives are imbued with, and built upon, such rounds. We shall return to this idea in more detail in later chapters. But for now it's enough to note that at certain **critical times of life** we inevitably find ourselves in the company of the dark man.

Attitudes and Qualities

As we have seen, the dark man often triggers attitudes and emotions such as **fear, loathing** and **terror** when he appears in a dream, story, etc. Thereby he is commonly associated with **danger** or even with **evil**. However, it is important to realise that the dark man himself is neither dangerous nor evil – 'evil' being something that sapient creatures are *capable of doing* and not an archetypal energy of the universe – but that he merely appears at times of change or when change is long overdue. In fact, the dark man serves to *liberate* us from that which is outworn, detrimental or evil, rather than embroiling us further into it. But again, more of this later.

Yet it is worth pointing out that in times past, when fear and loathing of the dark man was at its most apoplectic, it was certain powerful individuals who forwarded the view that the dark man was malevolent, diabolical or evil; and the fire and brimstone these people spat out was used to keep the masses in a state of passivity and servitude. After all, these powerful men did not want *their* subjects, *their* subservient, kowtowing, docile possessions, cohorting with anyone or anything that might undermine their authority or rock the status quo. Thus ordinary men were manoeuvred into positions of absolute compliance, and women, who are naturally associated with the dark man, were systematically humiliated, tortured, mutilated and murdered in an attempt to liberate both them and the land on which they lived from the darkness which is a natural part of all our souls. And be under no illusion, some of this behaviour may have had its roots in naïveté or religious misunderstanding, but by far and away the bulk of it was grounded in politics, money and power. What's more, even today, things haven't changed a whole hill of beans.

Anyhow, following on from this, we can say that the dark man is also associated with the states of **ignorance, limitation, torment** and **captivity**. But it is important to realise that, once again, the dark man does not actually hold us in these conditions but that he is, in fact, our way out of them.

The dark man is also said to have a **mesmeric** or **hypnotic** quality which enchants or entrances, draws us in or seduces us. And there are countless stories about naïve individuals who **sleepily** meander into dark untold dangers or inadvertently make a pact with a **charismatic** stranger and then find themselves up to their necks in more than they ever bargained for. Again, this does not make the dark man bad or evil, for, as Joseph Campbell noted, it is important that we follow *the Herald*, and, as Jung observed, sooner or later we must all enter the darkness. However, when the dark man is around we must endeavour to stay in a wide-awake, almost feral, state of consciousness; as although the dark man is our ally we still have to fight our own battles, and there really *are* leg traps and monsters down there in the darkness.

Nevertheless, there is an unfortunate tendency (especially among young women) to fudge the boundaries between the dark man and one of his archetypal neighbours and to thereby see him as something he is not. Again, we shall come back to this later. But for now it is enough to say that (a) the dark man should never be seen as an object of desire, as he is in fact **the antithesis of desire**, which is why it takes so much insight and courage to walk with him, and (b) it is extremely unwise for anyone to fall for the immature baloney regarding dalliances with dark strangers that tends to be put forward in certain types of novelette and which, in real life, seldom results in a happy ending. As Clarissa Pinkola Estés observes:

> When I work with older teenage girls who are convinced that the world is good if only they work it right it always makes me feel like an old gray-haired dog. I want to put my paws over my eyes and groan, for I see what they do not see, and I know, especially if they're wilful and feisty, that they're going to insist on becoming involved with the predator at least once

before they are shocked awake. [4]

But then again, she also observes that:

> In hindsight, almost all of us have, at least once, experienced a compelling idea or semi-dazzling person crawling in through our windows at night and catching us off guard. Even though they're wearing a ski mask, have a knife between their teeth, and a sack of money slung over their shoulder, we believe them when they tell us they're in the banking business. [5]

Paleness

In the same way that the 'darkness' that is associated with the dark man is more than just a colour, but is in fact a kind of *sensibility* invoking feelings and ideas of night, mystery, menace, etc.; so the concept of 'paleness' is far more than just a shade of white. In fact, although it is often described as the colour of **moonlight**, paleness is actually a **dull white** or a **sallow shade of off-white**, which is reminiscent of church candles without their waxy lustre. It is the total **absence of colour, light and life**. It is the empty shade of **death**.

The dark man often appears in association with that which is pale. For instance, we may see him in all-white surroundings, in the moonlight, or with a pale-coloured wolf or horse. And although the pale icons/creatures that appear alongside the dark man can be neuter or of either gender, they are, in fact, almost always *female*.

Then again, the dark man can embody the concept of paleness himself, and very many people do see him with **pale skin**. For example, in Angela Carter's *The Company of Wolves* the wolf-man's skin was said to be 'the colour and texture of vellum', [6] while the infamous 'Pinhead' in the *Hellraiser* films had dull white skin. Moreover, in our dreams, it is fairly common to see the dark man as absolutely, totally, **one single shade of pale**, so that his hair, face, clothes, etc. are all the same shade of dull off-white – though his eyes may be white, red or black. And, interestingly, although people usually say they are absolutely *terrified* of this **pale man**, on closer questioning it is often the case that he is not aggressive and that he is actually bringing *explicit* messages of help, reassurance or even compassion. However, this aspect of his character is often effaced from the film and storybook representations.

Yet, unfortunately, this is where we must leave 'the pale dark man' behind, for following him would be a journey in itself, and one that would take us way beyond the remit of this book. But for our purposes, all that we really need to remember is that the dark man is *associated* with the concept of paleness, and when pale objects and creatures appear alongside him they are typically female as opposed to the masculine gender embodied by his darker companions.

Where We Find the Dark Man

We have already come a long way and have almost finished padding out the abstract concept of the dark man into something that approaches a three-dimensional figure, and you may have begun to remember snippets from your dreams, daydreams, fantasies, nightmares and waking experiences where *you* actually brushed up against or *met* this entity. You see, far from being an abstract concept or a theoretical oddity, the dark man is a tangible element in all our lives, which, by virtue of us simply 'being here', we all experience from time to time. Indeed, you may now find it interesting and useful to make a note of your own dark man experiences.[7]

We have also touched on the idea that the dark man exists within a particular environment, which we may understand as underlying our own reality, and which can be accessed through – or which is a part of – our imagination and dreams. And in the next two chapters we shall broaden our understanding of the dark man by looking at this dream-world, or *Otherworld*, and examining his role within it. However, before we go on to look at the dark man in this wider context, I would like to linger just a little while longer in our own reality to consider some of the times, places, etc. where we are most likely to meet him.

As I mentioned earlier, many of the things that are associated with the dark man can act as 'portals' through which we can experience him and/or assess the state of our relationship with him. From a mystical point of view, these portals are said to occur at specific times and places where the fabric between our own world and the Otherworld is particularly thin; while from a more psychological perspective, it might be said that certain places, objects, etc. trigger our unconscious mind to respond in particular ways – which in this case involves it pitching insights and images of the dark man into our dreams and waking consciousness. Either way, it is indisputable that by thinking about, looking at, or going to certain places; contemplating certain objects; doing certain things; or even during specific times, we can invoke, tune into, or suddenly find ourselves in the company of the dark man.

Now, although the dark man is certainly not the most reassuring entity to be around, there are several reasons why we may want to meet him in this way. First, it allows us to familiarise ourselves with him under fairly neutral conditions, as opposed to the intense situations we are usually caught up in when he arrives spontaneously; and this gives us a better chance of responding to both him and those situations in a wide-awake responsible way, rather than with the muddle-headed decisions or knee-jerk reactions we might otherwise make. Second, it helps us be aware of our attitudes, beliefs and behaviours towards this hugely significant part of ourselves and our world; and this gives us the opportunity to work on any parts of the relationship that may not be functioning particularly well, before something really starts to go wrong. And third, it opens our eyes to the bigger reality within which we all live, work and play, and within which the dark man is just one (albeit significant) occupant, who influences us all to an extraordinary degree. So, with this in mind, we shall now take a look at some of the   situations, places and times where we are most likely to chance upon the dark man.

Dreams

Carl Jung held that our dreams are a rich source of archetypal experiences, while Clarissa Pinkola Estés claims that dark man dreams are so common it is surprising if a woman has reached age twenty-five without having had one.[8] Robert Graves also understood that the dark man, whom he knew as the 'Rival', comes to us in our dreams, while Joseph Campbell recognised that the archetypal cast of the monomyth spontaneously surface in dreams at various times in our life. Moreover, ancient myths and stories repeatedly tell of old gods coming to people while they slept; while, in the slightly different language of religion or religious enlightenment, there are numerous examples of angels and other divine messengers delivering pronouncements to sleeping people or to people who had just woken and were thereby in that awake-asleep hypnogogic state.

Yet, although dreams are one of the richest sources of dark man experiences, not all dreams that feature a shadowy dark figure are dark man dreams, as such. Indeed, most dreams are nothing more than a jumbled mishmash of the day's events, swirling around in our mind on their way to finding an appropriate home in our subconscious or unconscious psyche. This is not to say that such dreams are irrelevant or worthless, as we can learn a lot by observing the way our mind sifts and stores its information. It's just that true dark man dreams have a very different quality and exist on a very different level of profundity from these humdrum **little dreams**.

Generally speaking, little dreams tend to involve a jumbled

collection of images and experiences that are connected to each other in ways that make them difficult or awkward to recount on waking – that is, if we remember them at all for most little dreams tend to be forgotten moments after we open our eyes. In contrast, archetypal **big dreams** are much more real, with a greater feeling of depth and brighter colours. They are more coherent and often contain a definite storyline which can be recounted fairly easily. Also, the characters that appear in these dreams are very real, and we tend to feel a significant amount of emotion towards them (be it love, trust, fear, etc.). Moreover, big dreams almost always stay with us on waking. In fact, when we do wake up there is often a real sense of 'coming back' from somewhere a long, long way away. And for hours after, we may feel as if the dream is 'still with us', which can be a somewhat disorientating experience. Indeed, big dreams often remain fixed in our memory, as vivid as if they had happened only moments before, and they will often be recounted for *years* afterwards without alteration or embellishment, as if to tinker with them is somehow impossible or 'wrong'. Finally, big dreams can change our life. Maybe because of the intense emotions felt within them, or possibly due to the sense of profundity and insight they bring about, big dreams frequently open up new ways of looking at our self and the world which inevitably affects the way we think and the choices we make.

Therefore dark man dreams are big dreams. They are powerful, swelling, archetypal messages from deep within the roots of the mind and they offer us a wealth of insight into ourselves and our reality. Yet it is important to realise that there are various levels of 'bigness'. We can think of this as a sliding scale with the shallowest little dreams at one end, the biggest, deepest, most resonant big dreams at the other, and in between many steps connecting the two. In fact, it is common for a rich archetypal element to pop up in the middle of an otherwise little dream, whereupon this one element will be more real, more significant, and tend to be remembered long after the rest of the dream has disappeared into the ether. Indeed, this single element could comprise an important dark man experience in itself. However, the problem with these fragments is that they often require much more interpretation (i.e. more room for subjective slip-up) than big dreams *per se*.

A fairly typical example of a big dark man dream happened several years ago to a lady called Ruth. In the dream, Ruth was awakened by something out on the landing of her home. She wondered at first if it was her young daughter who had been ill earlier that night. So Ruth called out her daughter's name and then got out of bed to see that everything was all right. As Ruth walked across the landing towards her daughter's room something caught her eye: there was a hole in the ceiling at the top of the stairs. Shocked, Ruth walked towards the hole and looked up into the inky darkness of the roof space beyond. Icy air blew down from the hole and Ruth wrapped her dressing gown tightly around herself. It was then that Ruth got the feeling that she was being watched and, with her heart pounding in her chest, she forced herself to turn around, whereupon she saw, to her absolute horror, a tall, gaunt, swarthy-skinned man, with jet-black hair and dark clothes, silently staring at her from the other side of the landing. Worst of all were his eyes, which were so black it seemed that he was looking at her out of empty eye sockets. At first Ruth was too afraid to move, and when she tried to scream and call for help only dry little croaking noises came out of her mouth. However, the man then began to walk forward and Ruth's only thought became the safety of her daughter and her husband, so she lurched forward to try and force her way past the dark stranger, and it was at this point that she woke up in her own bed, with her heart pounding in her chest, tears pouring down her face and sweat soaking her body. It is also worth noting that at the time of the dream Ruth had just begun putting things in place to take a leap of faith and begin her own business. However, when I saw her two days later, tears still streamed from her eyes as she recounted the experience, and she told me that she *knew* the dream had something to do with her new venture and that she was giving it all up for fear of ever meeting this man again. And, true to her word, Ruth did give it up. And nine years later she is still living in a place she hates, making do with what she's got, and talking about what she might do if... when... eventually...one day... when she was so close to making a difference for herself and her family way back then.

Ruth's dream is a good example to look at because it is fairly representative of what we might call **a 'classic' dark man dream**, in that the string of elements it contains – night time, being alone, a dark assailant, an inability to call for help,[9] connotations of death and a spill-over into 'real' life – form the basis of many (if not most) dark man dreams. However, not all dark man dreams rigidly follow this classic pattern and when scanning our dreams for signs of the dark man it is worth bearing in mind the *characteristics and associations* that we looked at earlier. For instance, Gertie dreamed that she was trapped on a narrow girder[10] at the top of a tall skyscraper-like building which was under construction; and she was desperately trying to inch her way towards the relative safety of a platform which lay some way ahead, when a tall, dark figure stepped onto the platform and she didn't dare to continue. Likewise, Jackie dreamed that she was walking around a beautiful sunny house when she opened a door and found herself in a dark, filthy room with excrement dripping from the walls, furniture and ceiling.[11] Similarly, Rowan had a dream in which she was walking through beautiful emerald-green countryside when she came across an old railway tunnel that had a thick curtain of cobwebs over the entrance. As she pushed the cobwebs aside and stepped into the darkness Rowan reeled as a palpable atmosphere of death overwhelmed her. She couldn't see anything in the pitch blackness, but she knew that the tunnel was full of cadavers that had been hidden there by a terrible man who had murdered and mutilated countless innocent victims.[12] And then there was James, who was sound asleep in bed when he kept feeling a black shadow brush past him. In his dream James 'saw' the shadow as an intruder and he lay in bed planning a surprise attack against the nefarious man.[13] However, in the end, it was James's wife who was the most surprised as when, in the middle of the night, her husband sprang out of bed with a force that almost pushed her onto the floor.

Story
Stories and myths provide another rich source of dark man experiences. Admittedly, they don't tend to have the vividness or personal significance of dark man dreams, but they are still extremely relevant and they can pack a strong emotional punch. Moreover, stories are much more accessible than big dreams in that we don't have to wait for them to happen, but can instead turn to them whenever we choose. What's more, stories offer a vast spectrum of dark man guises to work with, as through the years poets, mythmakers, storytellers, novelists, film makers, etc. have depicted the dark man in a myriad of different ways, and this gives us the opportunity to set ourselves against a succession of men, animals, monsters, inanimate objects and challenging situations to test how we respond to the dark man's many different faces.

If we want to look for the dark man in stories, the first thing we need to do is identify a character in a fairytale, novel, film, etc. that embodies, or appears alongside, any of the character- istics and associations we looked at earlier. The next thing is to look closely at the thoughts, feelings, emotions and imaginative pictures that this character stirs up inside us. For example, do you feel intimidated by *the highwayman*? Does *the big bad wolf* revolt you? Does *Heathcliff* cause you to flatten your ears? Does *the Scissor Man* scare you when you are alone in the darkness? Or does *Dracula* stir up feelings of passion and lust? We shall return to the relevance of these different characterisations and the significance of our responses towards them in chapters 5 and 6 when we look at the dark man in relation to our own lives. But for now, it is enough to simply familiarise ourselves with this old archetype as he appears in countless different stories and begin to get an idea of how we respond to his many faces.

Wakeful Experiences
Dark man experiences that occur while we are in a wakeful state of consciousness are very common and can take place at different times and in a number of ways. They can happen when we are in the deeply relaxed **awake-asleep** state of mind that we pass through on the very edge of sleep or consciousness, and can be very dreamlike in nature or have an extremely mythological content – even in people who have *no previous knowledge* of the myths and mythological characters in question. They can happen when we are in the relaxed and receptive state of mind known as **reverie** or when we are **concentrating on a repetitive task**, such as driving a car or washing the dishes. And they can happen when we are fully alert, cogent and sober. And these truly **wide-awake** experiences can range from snatched glimpses of shadowy figures to unequivocally 'solid' encounters with the dark man in any of his forms – and you may be surprised at just how common these more 'solid' encounters really are!

Moreover, it seems that particular locations, such as **trees, water** and **darkness**, can trigger dark man experiences, while many other dark man encounters take place in our **home** (especially in the bedroom, kitchen, hallway and cellar) or when we are **driving**. This is probably because (a) we spend so much time in our homes and vehicles, and (b) while we are at home or driving we are more likely to be in the open relaxed state of mind conducive to dark man encounters. However, there may be another more esoteric reason why dark man **roadside encounters** are so common and it is that, as you may remember, the dark man is inextricably associated with paths and roads, and especially with places such as forks or crossroads where roads meet and *choices* have to be made.

For instance, what initially seemed to be a fairly typical roadside encounter happened several years ago to a young man called Matthew. It was a beautiful summer's day and Matthew was riding his motorcycle through the town where he lived. He was happy, relaxed and concentrating on the road when suddenly, in the corner of his eye, he caught sight of a very tall, black, shadow-like figure standing at the side of the road. Matthew whipped his head around to look at this figure, but as he did so the 'shadow man' disappeared, so, not thinking any more about it, Matthew continued on his way. However, when the same thing happened a couple of days later in a different part of town, Matthew was a little more unnerved. There was something about the figure that was 'not nice'. And when he next took his bike out on the open road Matthew just couldn't shake the memory of it or the feelings that it stirred up inside him; thus he was riding with a tad more care and attention than he might otherwise have done when a large four-wheel-drive vehicle came thundering around a blind corner on his side of the road. There was little Matthew could do, but, as he was especially focussed on his riding that day, the little that he did probably saved his life. And as he lay there in the hospital bed, broken, bruised and operated upon, Matthew was adamant that the dark figure, as 'not nice' as it was, had saved him because it was quite simply not his time to die.

In fact, stories like Matthew's, where a dark figure precedes **a traumatic event**, or else intervenes within it, are extremely common and are not limited to roadside encounters. For instance, a different kind of wakeful dark man occurrence is the **sickbed encounter,** whereby a person who is injured, poorly, awaiting surgery or otherwise caught up in a stressful and possibly life-threatening experience, reports seeing a dark visitor at their bedside. Like most other dark man encounters the visitor is typically tall, dark, quiet and male. Yet, in this instance, the dark man tends to deliver feelings of comfort and reassurance to the person and is often taken to be a doctor or some other authority figure. For example, when Caitlin began to experience difficulties during labour, and the obstetricians and midwives were hurrying to ready her for theatre, she clearly remembers lying there watching the tall, dark 'doctor' standing at the back of the room. She recalls having the unmistakable impression that this man was 'in charge' and that as long as he was with her everything would be all right. Yet, afterwards, when Caitlin asked after the 'doctor' so that she could thank him for taking care of her and her daughter, the confused midwives told her that no such person had been in the room or even worked at the hospital. And it was only then that Caitlin realised how strange it was that the 'doctor' had never spoken a word the entire time he had been in the room, but that he had just stood returning her gaze the whole time.

Of course, not all sickbed encounters have happy endings, and there are numerous stories of people being visited by the tall, dark character that most of us know as *Death* or *The Reaper*. What's more, such accounts cannot be dismissed as hokum or primitive superstition as these **'deathbed' encounters** *really do happen*. For instance, my very ill and all but bedridden ninety-three-year-old grandmother leapt out of bed one morning in a state of terror to go looking for my mother because 'the Devil' had appeared in her bedroom.[14] Similarly, when my neighbour's brother met the same figure in a dream, he *knew* – even to the point of tidying his house, arranging his will and telling his concerned sister where his important documents were kept – that he wouldn't survive a forthcoming operation. And, sure enough, following the operation, Peter never regained consciousness and he died shortly after due to complications. Yet, this said, it is vitally important to realise that by far and away *the vast majority* of dark man experiences are *not* portents of death, as such, but are in fact **promises of life** – as they were for Matthew, for Caitlin and her baby, and for countless other people as well. It's just that popular imagination has, typically enough, latched onto the most negative aspects of the phenomenon while simultaneously dismissing its positive aspects out of hand.

Nature

The dark man is intimately bound to nature or the natural world and we have already looked at a number of *environmental* places and situations that he is closely connected to and the *times* he is associated with. What's more, all these associations can be used to trigger dark man experiences in much the same way that the characters in stories can trigger our thoughts, feelings and dream experiences. Additionally, many of these places are also associated with dark man encounters of a more tangible kind. For example, in the middle of a tangled wood near where I used to live there was a large waterfall which fell into a deep, dark pool of still water. In the summertime, when the water levels were low, children would jump from the falls and enjoy swimming in the pool. Yet, at other times of year, the falls had a darker nature and unfortunately over the years a number of people had drowned at the spot and occasionally their bodies had never resurfaced. Indeed, on numerous occasions, the police and other people had used diving equipment to search beneath the falls in an attempt to discover what lay in the deep water. However, none of them had ever managed to reach the bottom of the pool as the water was too deep and dangerous for them to do so. Now, these falls would make an excellent subject for contemplation if we wished to explore our relationship with the dark man. However, the story doesn't end there as the woods, and especially the area around the falls, were also known for the strange otherworldly encounters that were said to occur there.

49

For example, *hobgoblins*[15] were regularly seen in the area and there were numerous reports of *a tall, blacker-than-black shadow* that moved along the path and between the trees. There were also accounts of a *tall, dark figure* that would stand silently and watch people as they approached or passed by. Though, of course, we would all do well to remember that scary men in tangled woodland are not necessarily of supernatural origin.

Thoughts and Behaviour
The dark man is *hugely* apparent within our thoughts and in our behaviour, both individually and on a collective level, and one of the places where he is most evident is in the **limitations and boundaries** that we put around ourselves and other people. These boundaries can take the *physical* form of walls, barriers or borders; they can be *abstract* as in the case of rules, laws and legislation; or they may be of a more *subtle* nature, such as the attitudes and values prevalent in our home, family, society or culture. And these subtle constraints are often the most pervasive of all.

Furthermore, throughout history certain individuals and organisations – be they police, army, leaders, teachers, family, etc. – have adopted or embodied a number of the dark man's more negative characteristics and associations, and have thereby risen into positions of power through sustained regimes of manipulation, coercion, destruction and terror; while the people they have had power over have increasingly found themselves forced to live limited lives within which all show of individuality, autonomy and freedom of thought and expression have been systematically sought out and slain. However, regardless of whether people are *consciously aware* of these violations or not, whenever such destructive forces start to impinge on our basic self the dark man will stir in our psyche and begin to step into our dreams, thoughts, feelings and intuitions with increasing urgency. As Clarissa Pinkola Estes observes: 'When the outer world has intruded on the basic soul-life of one individual or many, dark man dreams come in legions'. [16]

However, it must also be pointed out that those who ground their power on our fear of the dark man are actually building on sand, for the dark man is not concerned with our limitations and boundaries *per se* – they are ours and ours alone – but he is concerned with the *choices* that we make in regard to the limitations and boundaries that are placed around us. As they say, 'Rules are there to be broken'. And the dark man stands before every choice that we make in every waking moment of every day, asking us, 'Well, what are you going to do now?' **And the choices that we make** in such situations and **the way we see those choices through** are what lie at the *absolute centre* of the dark man phenomenon.

Now, we shall return to the subject of *choice* throughout the book, and especially in chapters 5 and 6 when we look at the dark man in relation to our own lives. But for now you may like to begin to consider how *you* approach the choices that *you* make in *your* life. For instance:

- do you trundle along, following well-worn *unconscious patterns of thought and behaviour,* so that it seems as if you are travelling on predetermined tracks of experience or are stuck in those proverbial ruts?
- do you make *conscious choices* about what to do next in your life? And if you do make conscious choices, do you see those choices through; do you repeatedly *fall short* of seeing your ideas to completion; do you *make excuses* so that you don't even have to begin; do you only choose ideas which *maintain the status quo* and so don't require any real commitment; or do you hide behind *excessive planning and analysis* instead of actually getting on with things?
- do you simply feel so *lost, alone and stuck* in your life that the mere idea of choice feels like an empty mockery?

As I said, just begin to feel out these options, to see which of them may be true for you in different areas of your own life.

In this chapter we have looked at the various forms the dark man can take and at the clothing, creatures, places, etc. that he is associated with and that are found alongside him. We have also considered some of the situations and places where the dark man can be found. And the outcome of this is that you should now be in a better position to recognise the dark man when he appears in your dreams, daydreams, etc. or when you come across him in stories, paintings, songs, films and so on. You should also be in a better position to appreciate the positive messages of reassurance and hope that the dark man can bring.

It has also been suggested that you make some notes about where, when and how the dark man appears to *you*, and that you may like to think about how you approach the *choices* that you make – or avoid making – in *your* life. We shall be returning to these points in later chapters.

Chapter 3

The Underworld

The dark man, whether we want to think of him as an old god, a law of nature, an archetype, or *whatever*, is a universal phenomenon that has been with us since the very beginning. He is in our myths, stories, dreams and waking life, where he may appear as a swarthy gentleman; a dark, debased creature; beneath a pallid moon; or in the company of a pale woman, mare or she-wolf. He may manifest as an aura of fear or anxiety, or as a terrifying dark presence. He is present in our patterns of thought and behaviour. He is inherent within the passing of time, the turning of the seasons and the whole of nature. And, if we know what to look for and how to listen, the dark man can be one of our staunchest allies, bringing messages of reassurance, promise, direction and hope. So much is pretty much unarguable – unless, of course, we choose to ignore thousands of years of human experience. The dark man quite simply *is*.

Yet, if we left our examination here, what we would be left with is the dark man as a kind of isolated curiosity – a bit like the planet *Pluto*, which does what it does at the very edge of our lives, while only those who are interested enough argue about what it is and document it as it passes by. Yet the dark man is no mere curiosity. He is a dynamic and imperative force within our lives – remember that Jung referred to the archetypes as *dominants* of the unconscious – and to understand how and why this is the case we must widen our examination to look at the dark man in the context of his immediate surroundings, or the place where he is found.

Where is the Dark Man Found?

Time and time again, the old stories tell of a dark mysterious stranger (or one of his associates) who is found beside a **hole, passageway, cave, tunnel** or **pool of dark water** that leads deep into the earth; or beside a **path, gate** or **bridge,** which leads to either a **fertile paradise,** such as the meadow on the other side of the river that lured the *Three Billy Goats Gruff,* or to a **dark, dangerous, claustrophobic environment,** such as underground caves, a labyrinth, a deep dark forest or an enchanted castle. Often the dark stranger is said to be the **gatekeeper** or **guardian** of these places, whereupon he may appear as a large dog, monster, beast, warden, gardener, or even as the Lord of the Dead. On other occasions he may be **opportunistically lurking** at their periphery, as was the Big Bad Wolf in the tale *Little Red Riding Hood.* Finally, the dark stranger is often said to present a **challenge** to the approaching hero or heroine, which may take place on the **threshold** of this strange land, at its **absolute centre** or at the **far gate** when the protagonist is tired, broken and ready for home.

The place that is being described here is none other than the fabled **Underworld,** or the dreadful Land of the Dead. And, as stories, myths, legends, dreams, creative insights and modern psychology all suggest, the dark man is intimately associated with this region. In fact, as many of the old tales reveal, the dark man is fundamentally *tied* to the Underworld – at least for the time being.[1] So, to broaden our understanding of the dark man, we must first consider what the Underworld might be, what it contains and what relevance it has to our own lives, before, in the next chapter, considering the role that the dark man occupies within it.

What is the Underworld?

If we think back to the idea of *laws of nature,* it becomes fairly easy to imagine that our universe and all that is in it 'rests on' a slice of reality that contains, or consists of, these fundamental laws and that these laws created and continue to give shape to all things. Similarly, if we choose to substitute 'laws of nature' for the entities we know as *old gods*, then this fundamental slice of reality becomes 'the home of the gods' and whether we call it *the Tuat, Olympus, Sidh, the Otherworld*, etc. it is from this region that the gods actively work to make and shape all that we know. Finally, if you feel more at home with a psychological approach, then the aspect of reality that gives shape to all things (or at least to our *perception* of all things) is *the unconscious mind*. So, following this, we can see that, however we may choose to ground the concept and whatever we may choose to call it, **the 'Otherworld' is quite simply the 'place' that underlies the universe as we know it and which continues to give shape to all that we know.**

Moreover, since the beginning of time, mystical and spiritual traditions have understood the Otherworld to be composed of two opposing but complementary halves which are typically represented as 'light and dark', 'day and night', 'male and female', 'heaven and hell', 'the Upperworld and the Underworld' and so on; while psychology makes a similar distinction between the 'lighter and darker' or 'higher and lower' aspects of the unconscious mind.[2] What's more, these two complementary halves are almost always recognised as embodying certain characteristics which are familiar to us from the world of biology. Thus the light half of the Otherworld is traditionally seen as *projective, rational* and *male*, while the dark side of the Otherworld is understood to be *receptive, intuitive, mysterious* and *female*.[3] And as we have already seen, the dark man, despite his obvious masculinity, is intimately tied to the dark side of the Otherworld, or **the Underworld**, and it is this link to *the feminine principle* which explains why he is often thought to be closely affiliated with women. Yet, as you can see, this is something of a misconception, as instead of women *per se*,

who after all embody a range of masculine and feminine characteristics (as do men), the dark man's affiliation lies solely with the
feminine. However, we should also note that, whether we like it or
not, the average woman does tend to embody more feminine
characteristics than the average man, and it is for this reason that
women are likely to approach the dark man differently from
men, who, as we have seen, are more inclined to react towards
the dark man with hostility and loathing.

Anyhow, what we can now say is that **the Underworld is the
dark, mysterious, 'feminine' side of the Otherworld,** and that
**the dark man's connection with the Underworld is mirrored in
his close association with the feminine.**

What the Underworld Contains

Having established what the Underworld is, the next thing to
think about is what it contains. After all, it must contain *something*
even if that something is just a bundle of probabilities, or laws of
nature, which have a tendency to manifest themselves in certain
ways in the everyday world. However, a problem with this is that
probabilities or natural laws are pretty abstract. Likewise, old
gods are rather incorporeal. Also, the deepest darkest roots of our
unconscious are, by definition, hidden from view. Nevertheless,
although we can't literally see the laws of nature/old gods/arche-
types themselves – in their true form, as it were[4] – we can
certainly observe the *effects* they have within our world and
especially in our *mind*, which I suppose picks up the effects of
these fundamental influences much faster than more solid objects
such as molecules, people, trees, etc.[5, 6] Anyhow, by entering *a
relaxed state of mind,* such as dream, reverie or calm concentration,
we can see the reflections of the Otherworld as they appear in our
imagination or our 'mind's eye'. And it's by entering these softer
states of mind that storytellers and other artists arrive at their
intuitive insights about the Otherworld and its inhabitants; it's
how deep and meaningful myths evolve; how psychological

analysis arrives at the source of our problems; how mystics and shamans enter the Otherworldly realms; and it also explains why so many dark man experiences occur while we are dreaming, daydreaming, driving and so on. Furthermore, once we look past the layers of creative embellishment and personal colouring to what people are actually saying about their 'Otherworldly' experiences, it becomes manifestly obvious that we are all experiencing *exactly the same thing*. In other words, people's observations, intuitions and testimonies all support the idea that the Otherworld is *an objective reality*.[7]

So if the Otherworld is an objective reality, what does its darker half contain? Well, we have seen that the old stories identify several different areas within the region of the Underworld, which we can broadly categorise as: *the threshold; the inhospitable land; the verdant oasis; the centre of death; the path home; and the far gate*. We have also noted some of the ways in which these places can be represented within a tale. For instance, the threshold may take the form of a hole, passageway, cave, tunnel or pool of water which leads deep into the earth, or a path, gate or bridge that leads to a different land. And, although the particular iconographic tokens can vary from story to story, even in modern tales the symbolism is pretty transparent with images such as a sliding door, a road barrier or a launch into outer space supplementing the more traditional symbols.[8]

Likewise, dreams and waking experiences also draw on a combination of traditional, contemporary and highly personal images, situations and experiences. Thus, while many people place a higher significance on conventional symbols – and indeed these can possess a more fundamental quality as well as having the weight of time and tradition behind them – we shouldn't dismiss the modern or the personal as meaningless, as the way our mind works is to colour its hidden contents with the most appropriate, or sometimes *the most readily to hand*, impressions it can muster.

Anyhow, from the insights offered by stories, myths, dreams, waking experiences, mysticism, shamanism, religion and psychology,[9] it seems that as we make our way through the Underworld the regions that we pass through can be described as follows.

1. *The threshold*: This marks the boundary between light and dark (i.e. our own world and the Underworld) and is commonly seen as an **entrance into the earth** (e.g. a cave or tunnel; a **threshold, boundary or barrier** into a different land (e.g. a doorway or bridge); some other **obstacle, difficulty or challenge** to be overcome; or as the **introduction of a dark, threatening, disruptive someone or something** into our pleasant, humdrum or stagnated lives.

2. *The inhospitable land*: This lies just beyond the threshold and is commonly seen as a **dark, claustrophobic and possibly dangerous environment** (e.g. a dark forest, underground caves or a labyrinth); as a **barren, hostile, 'dead' landscape** (e.g. a rocky mountainside, volcanic landscape or an arid desert); or as a **dark, cold and icy place**.

3. *The verdant oasis*: This is situated in the middle of the Underworld (i.e. in the middle of the dark forest etc.); is commonly seen as some sort of **blessed refuge** (e.g. an inn, a garden, a gingerbread house or Granny's cottage); and is often **surrounded by a barrier of some kind** (e.g. a fence, a wall, a high hedge or a river).

4. *The centre of death*: This is situated in the absolute *dead centre* of the Underworld (i.e. in the centre of the verdant garden, Granny's cottage, etc.) and it can take various forms that are almost always associated with **death, darkness or hell**. So the centre of death might be a trapdoor, a secret room, a fiery hot oven, a cauldron or cooking pot, or a dark creature sitting on a bed or wrapped

around a tree; while in modern tales it may be described as a black hole, a terrible weapon, a mother-alien's lair and so on.

5. *The path home*: Directly after the centre of death we find ourselves back in the verdant oasis (garden, cottage, etc.), only this time there is a **path, track or road** leading out of the oasis and back to our 'home'. This path is often seen to pass through pleasant woodland, but it may take us back across the arid desert or icy landscape of the inhospitable land, though this time the journey will be neither frightening nor hard. And one of the most notable things about this part of the Underworld is **the light**, which we may see as either a dawning sun or a warming golden glow. However, by the time the traveller has reached this stage of the journey he or she is typically **tired, broken** (e.g. scarred, wounded, or emotionally crushed) and **longing for home**, and so may fail to appreciate the relative pleasantness of the surroundings.

6. *The far gate*: At the very end of the path home lies the far gate. It is the threshold between darkness and light (i.e. the Underworld and either our own world or the Upperworld[10]) and we have to pass through it in order to arrive back home. It is typically seen as a **way out of the darkness** (e.g. a cave mouth); a **boundary or threshold into the light** (e.g. a door or a bridge); or as **waking from a long sleep**. Moreover, the far gate is often (but not always) a relatively unassuming structure. Yet it can present the most difficult challenge of all.

So what we have here is a pretty detailed outline of the Underworld, or the lay of its land, and, as you might have realised, it's an outline that is repeated again and again in countless, myths, legends, stories, poems, plays, films and even computer games. This isn't surprising really, as the Otherworld, its characters and the times and tides that govern it are what lie at the heart of Robert Graves' 'Theme', Joseph Campbell's 'monomyth' and all 'true' stories, which incorporate the theme (in whole or in part and with differing levels of skill and subtlety) into their narratives.[11] And the effect of writing, reading, telling, hearing or seeing one of these tales is a sense of aptness, satisfaction or even profundity, which is due to the fact that the Otherworldly landscape and the characters that are found within it lie at *the very roots of who and what we are*, and, possibly, *of all that is*. Therefore stories, poems, etc. that are congruent with the theme instil a feeling of *flow* or *rightness* within us, while those which go against it provoke a sense of *discord, wrongness* or *chaos*.

Now, as I have already suggested, the Underworld is home to a number of different characters or beings, each of which is coloured by the effects of our cultural, social and personal experiences. Thus, when we approach, say, the centre of the Underworld, we may find ourselves in the company of *Granny*, the *Wicked Witch* or the *Mother Alien*. So, once again, it is important to look beyond the surface particulars to the fundamental energies that lie below. What's more, like the dark man, all these characters have several ways of presenting themselves, numerous characteristics and associations, and their own particular agendas. And although all these characteristics, associations, etc. can't be listed here – we just don't have the space – what we can do is note the basic outline of these energies and entities, which we can then use to orientate ourselves as we make our way through the darkness. Thus, when we are making our way through the Underworld, we are likely to meet the following individuals.

1. *The threshold*: As we have already seen, whether he appears as a mysterious stranger, door-warden, bridge-keeper, ferryman, large black dog, the Devil, Death, etc. the **dark man** is always found at the threshold into the Underworld.

2. *The inhospitable land*: This region of the Underworld actually contains many different entities, but the ones most relevant to our purposes are **wild animals, strange beings and monsters**, which can be good, kind, helpful, ailing or sorrowful (e.g. the seven dwarfs, Mr Tumnus, Scarecrow, Tinman or Lion), or nasty, mean and malevolent (e.g. trolls, goblins, rapacious beasts or grasping trees). We may also chance upon a **being of light** in this region, which will be either female or androgynous, and which will manifest along the lines of a guardian spirit, high elf or fairy queen, and whose home is the inhospitable land itself. And at some point we will meet the **invisible guide, guardian or watcher**, who at first may be feared or reviled, but who will leave clues along the path and/or instil a sense of security and direction in us as we make our way along.

3. *The verdant oasis*: This area of the Underworld may be **empty of other human beings** (e.g. the enchanted castle in *Beauty and the Beast*); it may contain **sleeping people** (e.g. the castle in *Sleeping Beauty*); it may be seen as the home of an **older woman**, who is often described as someone's mother; and – and this is a contentious point which we shall come back to in the next chapter – it may also be seen as the home of, or a place tended by, a **male figure** who is typically dark, and who may have animal tendencies or characteristics.

4. *The centre of death*: This part of the Underworld comes under the jurisdiction of an old woman or the **oldest woman**, who is typically said to be dark and terrible, and who is variously described as a witch, the old queen, the enchantress, the thirteenth fairy, the mother alien and so on. And, once again, there is the contentious issue of masculinity within this part of the Underworld, with a **dark male creature** (e.g. a rapacious wolf or a cunning

serpent) or a **pale man** sometimes said to exist here, but, again, we shall come back to this in chapter 4.

5. *The path home*: This part of the Underworld is home to a **lady**, who is almost always associated with a bright, clear shade of blue, silver or silver-white; is kind, benevolent, gracious and pure; and is often portrayed as a godmother, a fairy godmother, or some other guide, guardian or protector. Many different **animals** are also found in this region, but they are always gentle and helpful. And birds (particularly doves, swans and bluebirds), white ponies and little donkeys are especially common.

6. *The far gate*: At the far gate we once again find ourselves in the company of **the dark man,** only this time he may be as terrifying as ever, or he might be older, more approachable, vulnerable or possibly ailing in some way.

This comprises a pretty detailed outline of the lay of the Underworld's land and the people and creatures you are likely to meet in each region. Though please remember that it is just an *outline*, which means that you will still have to use your insight and imagination to interpret what you see in stories, dreams, etc. And remember that what you do see will be coloured by images and experiences from your own life. For example, I once dreamed that I was outside a dark nightclub, wearing a beautiful silver dress, waiting for a car to take me home. When I woke from this dream I was filled with a sense of gladness and I knew that, for me, the nightclub represented the abyssal centre; the silver dress was symbolic of 'the lady'; and the car would be literally taking me 'home'.[12] In other words, this dream was a sign that I was on my way out of the darkness, and indeed, a few weeks later some things that I had been working on for quite some time suddenly and miraculously fell into place and life certainly did begin to move on. Similarly, a friend recently told me that she dreamed she was walking down a long dusty path in Italy under a beautifully warm sun which bathed everything in a beautiful golden light, and that a woman wearing a blue dress covered in little, round, light-reflecting mirrors was acting as her guide. In the dream my friend wanted to dawdle and return to a place she had visited some time before and the woman agreed, but said that my friend would have to return home on Friday, Saturday or Sunday. As my friend recalled, when she woke from this dream she was initially disorientated as she really thought that she was in Italy, but this was quickly followed by a sense of thankfulness and hope which stayed with her for much of the day. Therefore, in my friend's dream, we see the different motifs of the path through a foreign land, the warming light, and the blue and silver lady acting as guide. So, despite their apparent differences, both these dreams are archetypal 'coming home' dreams.

The Passage Through the Underworld

What we have discovered so far is that the Underworld is a place or situation that underlies the universe as we know it; we can see into the Underworld by entering softer, more relaxed states of mind, such as dream or reverie; the Underworld has its own topography and is populated by a number of distinct personalities; and it seems that the Underworld and our day-to-day lives correspond, or reflect, one another, in that as we experience ourselves in different regions of the Underworld, these experiences are paralleled by – or *slightly pre-empt* – the circumstances of our everyday life.

In a way, the fact that dreams and Otherworldly experiences can sometimes foretell our everyday experiences isn't too surprising, for, as we have already seen, the contents of the Otherworld (which we may understand as laws of nature, old gods, etc.) *make and shape* all that we know. Thus, when we have a big archetypal dream or enter a state of reverie, what we are actually witnessing is how the building blocks of our life, and possibly the world, are structured at that particular moment.

What's more, as the Otherworld is responsible for maintaining the shape of the material world, then, as we saw above, there is bound to be some sort of lag between cause and effect, as atoms, molecules, people, etc. need time to reorganise themselves in a way that is congruent with the underlying structure. Thus on some occasions our dreams may indeed *predict* changes that are destined to occur in the near future. And, incidentally, this is how *signs* (as in 'symbols of portent' or 'serendipitous omens') work.

Now, while the mystically minded will have no problem with the idea that on a deeper level we are moving through the Underworld and that the effects of this transit are seen in our dreams and day-to-day life, there may be other more materially minded individuals that are not so comfortable with the claim. However, for these people I will point out that so far in this book we have never once strayed from the idea that the dark man phenomenon may be a wholly corporeal experience and that what we might be seeing could 'simply' be the basic configuration of our world as it is reflected, or interpreted, by the archetypal contents of our psyche. What's more, in this instance the mystical–material division doesn't really count for much as the bald facts demonstrate that human beings have been experiencing the dark man and his companions and associations for thousands of years, and that people with the talents and/or skills have actively worked – and still work – with this level of reality on a regular basis.[13] Thus, once again, it doesn't really matter what we choose to call the dark man or how we prefer to rationalise him, for the facts are that gods and monsters, the Upperworld and the Underworld, the dark man, the 'wicked' witch, the benevolent 'lady', etc. do exist. They quite simply *are*.

Now, let us return to the idea that we are all, on some level, moving through the Underworld. In a way this is pretty self-evident, as if the dark man is found on the threshold of the Underworld, and if we are in the company of the dark man, then we too must be on the threshold of the Underworld. Likewise, if we subsequently experience being in a tangled forest or meeting a chimerical beast or a malevolent troll, then it seems reasonable to assume that we have passed into the inhospitable land. Therefore by being alert to these experiences we can use the landscape and inhabitants of the Underworld as way-markers or reference points to help orientate ourselves as we move through the darkness. However, if you are *really* not happy with the idea that we literally pass through the Underworld, then think of it as a metaphor for a natural cycle that takes place *inside us* (such as a developmental cycle or a biorhythm). As once again, the stance we adopt towards the ontology of this issue isn't as important as recognising that it actually occurs.

The Old Idea of Moving Through
The idea that we periodically pass through the darkness is as old as humankind itself. Maybe it began when people who lived closer to nature than we do now noticed that the natural world never stands still, but is always in a state of flux between life and death, or light and dark. These people might also have recognised that their own lives were filled with similar natural cycles, from the big one that took place between their own birth and death, to smaller twelve-year, annual, monthly, daily, even momentary cycles. They probably also recognised that the ebb and flow of these cycles corresponded to the insights and intuitions about dark men, benevolent ladies, monsters, etc. that came to them in their dreams and quiet moments. Thus stories were told, mythologies developed, belief systems shaped, ideologies contested and wars fought over a handful of... well... whatever.

Anyhow, the idea that we periodically move through the Underworld has a long, long history, and it was often transmitted, explained or ritualised using some sort of story, drama and/or visual imagery, which was sometimes deceptively simple and at other times ridiculously obscure or complex, as was often the case when it was embedded into 'mystery schools', secret societies, natural philosophies and religious systems. However, one very easy way to understand the passage through the Underworld is to think of yourself as sitting on the rim of an old, spoked cartwheel (⊛), which is half in shadow and half in light (◑), and which is slowly turning in an anti-clockwise direction. Now to begin with, you are at the very top of this wheel, but as it slowly turns you begin to move downwards (i.e. **fall**) towards the darkness until you arrive at the bottom of the wheel and enter the shadow... whereupon you immediately begin to **rise back up** to the top where you re-enter the light. And it is this transit from the bottom of the wheel back to the top, during which you are *travelling to meet the light head on* as opposed to following its path, which is analogous to the journey through the Underworld and is symbolic of the **passage of death back to life, resurrection or rebirth**.

Not all traditions used the symbol of the **wheel** to illustrate the passage through the Otherworld, though. Some used the **spiral pathway**. Some used an **ascending helix**. And some combined these two images, pulling the centre of the spiral upwards to make a cone shape, while speaking of the **ascending path** or the **path up the mountain**. Alternatively, some traditions split the Otherworld on *a horizontal axis* (◓), whereupon the Underworld was usually seen to be below the ground and the Upperworld above it in the skies. Yet, as it is a lot easier for human beings to fall over than it is for them to fly up into the sky, in the horizontally divided Otherworld the idea of *moving through* was often (but not always) lost, and people were instead told that they were tied to the Underworld/the feminine/the darkness/the material world/Hell and that their souls could only enter the Upperworld after they had died – and only then if they had been 'good'. However, not all traditions that split the Otherworld along a horizontal axis subscribed to this view, and **solar boats and chariots** were two of the devices that people and the gods were said to use in order to traverse the skies.[14]

Still, despite these differences in interpretation, there were some things that almost all the old traditions did agree on. First, they held that the journey through the Underworld was *a treacherous passage* and a time of danger and trial. Second, they recognised that it was a *necessary* journey to make. And third, they understood that *all things* must *periodically* pass through the darkness in order to maintain balance within the individual and the world. However, all too often the second and third of these insights were forgotten, misunderstood or sacrificed for the sake of greed, elitism or political ambition; and this resulted in disorder and a derangement of the self and the world that most of us are still living with today.

What Happens to Us as We Pass Through?
In the same way that a gyroscope must spin in order to maintain its equilibrium, so the whole of nature, from the smallest atom to the largest galaxy, must spin around and around to maintain its balance and harmony and to continue to exist. Everything moves in circles. Nothing can slow down or stop for long.

It's the same with us. Just because we can't see ourselves moving around, this doesn't mean we are standing still. After all, we can't see the Earth turning on its axis or orbiting the sun, but we can certainly experience *the effects* of these cycles when the sun rises in the morning and falls back to Earth at night, or when spring turns to summer, turns to autumn, turns to winter. Once upon a time people didn't understand why such things happened, but they did recognise a correlation between the events and their own insights and intuitions of old gods, spirits, etc. whom they took to be responsible for the phenomenal occurrences. Similarly, many people today are unaware that on some level of mind, body, spirit or soul we are moving around and around the Otherworld. Yet, although most of us are ignorant of the actual passing of this cycle, we can still take note of *the effect* it has on our day-to-day life, and even if we can't rationalise the hows, whys and wherefores of what is happening, we can still work with the insights of gods, monsters, etc. that it brings about.

In chapter 4 we shall be taking a closer look at the part of the Otherworldly cycle that takes us through the Underworld, and in chapters 5 and 6 we'll be considering the effect this transit can have on our lives. However, for now it will be useful to bear in mind that the time spent in the dark half of the Otherworld is essentially a period of **rest, healing and growth,** though we don't always experience it as such.

In fact, the association between darkness and rest is fairly obvious. After all, most of us work in the daytime and sleep at night, while the earth sprouts and grows in the sunny seasons, and ripens and rests as darkness reasserts itself. Therefore, the time we spend in the Underworld can be seen as a time of **enforced rest,** which in our day-to-day life is often mirrored by the **frustration** we feel as we find ourselves **unable to do or achieve almost anything.** Time stands still in the Underworld (think of Sleeping Beauty's enchanted castle), and although we may be craving to further our life and ambitions it can seem that **fate is against us** at these times. **Nothing works and we get nowhere fast.** So if ever you feel that **luck has left you** then be alert to the fact that on some level, and in some area of your life, you have probably entered (or got yourself stuck in) the Underworld.

Yet this said, it would be a mistake to think that *nothing* happens in the Underworld, for a great deal of **healing** takes place while we are in the darkness. For instance, as we make our way through the Underworld we have the opportunity to repair any *soul loss* or *soul distortion* that may have occurred at an earlier time.

Very simply, **soul loss** occurs when a bit of our soul or psyche splinters off, or is pushed down into the darkness of the deep unconscious. It is usually caused by trauma of some kind, and is comparable to Freud's idea of repressing difficult memories into the 'id', or to Jung's notion of burying parts of our self in the 'shadow'. Yet while we are making our way through the darkness we have the opportunity to recover and reintegrate these disassociated parts of our being and thus recover our *wholeness* or *selfhood*, which is incidentally the goal of psychotherapy and some shamanic practices. But we should also note that not everything that gets pushed down into the darkness is sinister, disturbing or 'bad'. In fact, there really are buried treasures down there, such as repressed talents, motivations and dreams; and in the language of folktale, fairytale and fantasy these nuggets are the *treasures, useful things* or *magical items* that the hero picks up along the way.

Similarly, **soul distortion** occurs when parts of the soul or psyche are pulled out of shape by our experiencing *negative or improper* events which have the effect of colouring our archetypes in increasingly misshapen ways and thereby warping our perceptions. On the surface such distortions can manifest in a range of unhealthy ways, such as a distorted sense of our own abilities or limitations, or a deep-seated and possibly all-consuming fear of, say, illness or personal attack. And in the language of fantasy, myth and magic these distortions are often represented by the monsters, demons or evil spirits that the hero has to overcome on the way to reaching his or her goal, and they also account for some of the antisocial *excesses* said to be enjoyed by old gods such as *Ares* or *Hera*.

Finally, and perhaps most fundamentally, the time we spend in the Underworld is a period of **growth**. Apparently babies and children do most of their growing while they are asleep. Similarly we, as adults, do most of our psychic or emotional growing while we are in the Underworld. Indeed, on emerging from the darkness, people often comment that it is as if they have acquired a whole new perspective on life and that that which once seemed problematic now seems simple or even irrelevant.

Thus these people have arrived at a whole new level of **maturity** from which to live out the next phase of their lives. But don't be fooled into thinking that the passage through the Underworld is 'simply' a matter of emotional growth, for biological stages of development, such as puberty and menopause, also mark the passing of the soul or psyche into the darkness. Thus the passage through the Underworld is *a holistic experience* with mind, body, spirit and soul all bound together in the process.

Must We Make this Passage?
If we return to the idea of a gyroscope which must spin in order to retain its balance and not wobble and fail, so the whole of nature must continually move through certain **natural cycles** if it is not to become distorted, dangerous or fall into chaos. And the key word here is *move*, for if anything does slow down, stutter or stop – and we with our complex minds and free will are particularly susceptible to this – nature will try to nudge it back into line before it surely ceases to be.[15]

In chapter 6, we shall look at some of the ways we might resist, or get stuck within, the Underworld and some of the ways in which nature tries to nudge us back onto the path. However, for now it is worth pointing out that as the galaxies spin, the heavens roll, the years turn, the months pass and the days go by, it doesn't really matter whether we view nature as a giant clockwork edifice composed of wheels within wheels within wheels, all clicking and ticking around one another in a regimental Newtonian order, or whether we see it as a matrix of holistically interconnected pathways which contain and reflect one another as a unified body. The fact is that allowing ourselves to stutter or stick in any part of the Otherworld, no matter how challenging or delightful this region may seem to be, is simply not a good idea for us personally, for our friends and family, for the places and things we love or for the rest of creation. You see, nature is very large and we are very small, therefore if we try to disrupt the balance of things we will *always* lose the fight. It's only ever a matter of how much damage we manage to do to ourselves and everything we hold dear along the way. So for this reason alone we *must* remain fluid, flexible and alert to our surroundings and pass through the Underworld whenever the times and tides are right for us to do so.

Moreover, although many transits of the Underworld are more or less predestined, in that we can't stop the night from falling nor remain a child forever, we also have a responsibility to enter the darkness at fairly regular intervals of our own *free will*. In other words, we must **choose** to heal, grow and develop as a human being, as opposed to simply functioning as a biological organism. It is the difference between *living* and *existing*. And it is also the reason why knowledge of the dark man has been warped or obscured by certain influential parties who have never wanted the people to think and act for themselves, for, as mentioned earlier, the dark man threatens the status quo, and throughout history there have been people with a vested interest in keeping us in our place and things pretty much as they are. So for this second more personal reason, it is *vital* that we choose to pass through the Underworld again and again throughout the course of our life.

Yet the problem with this is that the Underworld is a hard and hostile environment, so we need to have a damned good reason for choosing to enter it – which is something we shall return to in chapter 4. Moreover, the passage through is a hugely unpredictable journey to make, for although ancient disciplines such as astrology and numerology aim to help us understand the cycles of life, we can never really be sure how hard or how deep into the darkness any particular transit will take us. For instance, sometimes we may only need to step lightly into the shadowlands to pull a bit of the self back into realignment, while at other times we might have to negotiate the yawning abyss before we can find our way back to the light. Fortunately, the really hard, deep passages are relatively rare, but even in the 'easier' transits of the Underworld there is a real risk of losing one's self in the darkness and a person can suddenly find themselves faced with *a lot more* than they are able to cope with on their own. And this is where the dark man comes in, for this 'loathsome' creature, whom so many of us try to run from, fight against or ward off, is, as I have said, one of our truest allies. He is our way into the darkness, our guide through it and *our way home.*

What Lies on the Other Side?
After all this talk of 'passing through' the Underworld, you may have begun to wonder what lies in wait for us on the other side. After all, 'the far gate' must lead somewhere, but is that somewhere worth the effort of a journey through the darkness?

We shall return to this subject in later chapters, but for now we can note that as we travel through the Underworld, resting and repairing our soul loss and soul distortions, we are striving towards increasing *wholeness or completeness.* Thus it can be said that whenever we exit the Underworld we are arriving at **a new level of growth and maturity**.

However, while this is certainly a worthwhile outcome, it may seem a tad indefinite for some people – a bit like the holy grail of 'enlightenment', which is a splendid idea in principle but of little use when it comes to paying the bills. Yet there are other more tangible benefits waiting for us beyond the far gate, for, as we have seen, the passage through the Underworld is *a holistic experience* with mind, body, soul and spirit bound together in, and affected by, the transit. Thus, even if the passage through the Underworld primarily does take place on a deeper level of being, we should still expect to see the effects of the journey in our everyday life. And indeed we do, for the dark man is fundamentally connected to the notions of *dreams come true, answered prayers* and *granted wishes* – which are not synonymous concepts. So, in a very literal sense, what we find on the other side of the

Underworld is nothing less than **our heart's desire** or **happily ever after**. But, again, more of this later.

Finally, perhaps the most important thing that waits for us beyond the far gate is **home**. Now *home* is a difficult concept to put into words, but very many people live their lives with a feeling of deep loss and a sense of longing for something or somewhere they cannot explain or even bring to mind, except to know that it is the 'place' where they are *totally loved, totally accepted* and where they *totally belong*. Some people call this place 'heaven'. Some take it to be a state of completeness. And very many people spend their lives looking for 'home' in the material world: chasing rainbows in the hope that one day they will find what it is they are actually looking for. Yet, whatever we take it to be, we can be sure that each time we step out of the darkness we are one step nearer to this place of peace, love and harmony that many of us intuitively know as *home*.

What we have seen in this chapter is that the Otherworld is the 'place' that underlies the universe as we know it; that it continues to give shape to all that we know; and that although the laws/gods/archetypes that populate the Otherworld are invisible to our eyes, we can certainly observe *the effects* they have on our world, and especially on our mind, as by entering softer states of consciousness such as dream, reverie or calm concentration we can see coloured projections of them as they appear in our imagination or mind's eye.

We have also seen that the Otherworld is almost always understood to be composed of two opposing but complementary halves, which are usually represented as light and dark, male and female, the Upperworld and the Underworld etc. And that the dark man, who is often associated with features such as caves, tunnels, forests, etc. is essentially tied to the dark, feminine side of the Otherworld, or *Underworld*, which incidentally explains the (slightly mistaken) idea that he is closely associated with *women*.

Finally, we also noted that the Underworld has a specific topography, which is composed of six distinct regions that we must regularly pass through as we navigate the natural cycles that maintain the harmony and balance of our world. And we saw that each region is populated by a specific character (or characters) who might challenge or assist us as we move along, and who can be used – along with any topographical features that we recognise – to orientate ourselves as we make our way through the darkness.

So with this basic outline of the Underworld in place, we shall now turn our attention back to the dark man and take a look at precisely *what* he is doing down there in the darkness and, somewhat contentiously, *why* he might be doing it.

Chapter 4

The Lord of the Underworld

The dark man is fundamentally associated with the Underworld: the dark mysterious realm of the archetypal feminine. Indeed, the old myths tell us that Anubis, Hades, Lucifer, etc. were all chthonian deities. What's more, the old stories confirm that the dark man, by whatever name he went, was a *functional* part of the Otherworldly landscape: he had a *job* to do down there in the darkness. So in this chapter we shall take a look at *what* that dark man's function or job is and *why* he might doing it.

However, before we continue, just a word of warning. You see, as we begin to examine what that dark man does, it will become increasingly difficult to maintain an objective written stance towards him. For instance, when describing how he interacts, it is difficult not to use words like 'greets' and 'guides' even though such words clearly describe the actions of a conscious being, such as an old god, as opposed to the mechanical effects of a law of nature. Moreover, the problem compounds when we consider *why* the dark man does what he does, for the question 'why' usually entails that a reason be given and, once again, conscious beings give reasons for their actions, while laws of nature simply do what they do in a mechanical way.

Yet, in all fairness, we should also note that whenever people encounter the dark man they invariably *do* experience him as an attentive, responsive, perceptive personality. And although this in itself does not *prove* that the dark man is a conscious entity, it certainly makes it very difficult for most of us to talk about him as if he is not. Furthermore, when we consider *why* the dark man does what he does, then I invite anyone who does not believe he is a conscious being to simply take what they read as a metaphor for the ways in which laws of nature – or universal archetypes – interact. After all, nothing occurs in isolation. Except possibly God, that is.

The First Encounter

Literally speaking, we first encounter the dark man in early childhood when we first become aware of the archetype within our psyche. And although the manner in which the archetype first presents itself is necessarily coloured by our individual life experiences – especially our exposure to fear, limitation, shadow and death – to begin with it seems that many children intuit the dark man's attributes within particular *colours, shapes* and *situations*: the colours black and deep purple, the darkness and areas of deep shadow being particularly common. Then, as the child's life experiences become progressively more sophisticated, the archetype typically takes the form of *an animal* or *an artefact*, or it may be discerned within certain *places*: for instance, large black dogs which appear in dreams or playtime reverie are practically ubiquitous, while claustrophobic, dark places such as wardrobes, storerooms or cellars are often seen as frightening, fascinating or both. Finally, as the child develops further, the archetype takes on *human-like* or *human* forms. And it is important to note that for many young children dark man experiences are *positive* occurrences. For instance, I clearly remember feeling a mixture of reassurance and awe when the dark man appeared, and it wasn't until I was about five or six years old, probably after experiencing the pressures of school and the awfulness of some early evening news stories, that my dark man experiences began to take a negative turn. But, even then, the dark man didn't become wholly negative. It was just that the terrible side of his personality carried the stronger emotional clout and it was these negative emotional responses that tended to eclipse many of his more positive features.

So, at this early stage in our life, the dark man picks up or absorbs images and experiences from our everyday world which happen to reflect or resonate with his fundamental nature. Thus, on the positive side, he begins to appear as **a powerful, reassuring, protective-type figure, who imbues us with feelings of fortitude and companionship, and who helps us develop an almost feral sense of intuition regarding what is going on around us.** After all, the dark man is a somewhat bestial character who lives in the darkest of places. And this is why, if we choose to develop our relationship with him, we gain the ability to discern what lies beneath the surface of things.

Yet, at the same time, we may also come into contact with a more negative side of the dark man's character, in that he may begin to appear as **a dreadful creature, a terrible marauder or in some other threatening form.** And what is happening here is that the archetype is simply picking up on the images and associations connected to any fears and limitations we may be experiencing *on a conscious or unconscious level* in our own lives. And it is vitally important to realise that this does not happen because the archetype is 'bad' or 'evil', but because bad and evil things are happening in our world. These things may be going on around us: to people we know, to society, to the landscape, to other living creatures or to the world in general. Or they might be inflicted upon us: our liberties may be restricted, our humanity undermined or our spirit crushed.[1] But either way, whether we are consciously aware of the situation or not, **when fear and limitation enter our lives the dark man takes up these concerns and reflects them back at us.** In other words, the Lord of the Underworld shows us the 'monsters' so we can protect ourselves, deal with the dangers, and then move on in our lives.

However, the problem with this is that small children seldom have the capacity to deal with such difficulties. So, naturally enough, they turn to their parents or other significant adults to protect them and teach them how to handle the issues. Yet the parents seldom know much more than the child, so they call the dark man *a devil*, *a demon* or *an evil spirit*, in which case the child learns to fear fear itself, or they say that he is *just a nightmare* or *a figment of the imagination*, whereupon the child learns to marginalise and mistrust his or her own psyche. As parents all we have to do is take our children's fears seriously enough and show them how to deal with the dangers they perceive in their world. But as adults we are often afraid of precisely the same things as our children, and as we have never learned to deal with the darkness ourselves, how can we possibly pass such information on?

The Threshold

As mentioned in the last chapter, life is composed of cycles, very many of them, spinning and turning around us and within. From the passing of the seasons, to the way civilisations rise and fall, to our own progress through the various stages of childhood, maturity and old age, these cycles are *everywhere*. Wheels within wheels within wheels, they roll and revolve like a colossal natural mechanism that some have likened to the workings of a traditional pocket-watch. Yet regardless of whether 'the watch-maker' is an intelligent being endowed with reason and foresight, or whether the whole caboodle is 'simply' the product of a few blind dynamics, the one thing we can be *absolutely certain* of is that on each and every transit of each and every cycle, at the precise moment when light and life meets darkness and death, the dark man will be standing on the threshold to the Underworld waiting to meet us anew.

In fact, threshold encounters are by far and away the most common of all dark man experiences. They are what Joseph Campbell was referring to when he spoke of meeting the dark 'herald'. They are probably what Robert Graves was experiencing when he dreamed of 'the Prince of the Air'. And they correlate with much of what Clarissa Pinkola Estés says about dark man experiences. Also, images and accounts of such encounters abound within folktales, fairytales, poetry, paintings, literature, popular writing, cinema, and probably every other kind of creative art known to man. And they are almost always what adults are experiencing when they have a dark man encounter.

Moreover, as threshold encounters occur at one specific point of the natural cycle, and as the ebbs and flows of the natural cycle are reflected in the times and tides of life, we can be pretty certain that whenever we experience a dark man threshold encounter we are also caught up in a particular type of day-to-day experience. In fact, as the storytellers, mythographers, poets and psychologists that we looked at in chapter 1 observed, dark man threshold encounters always occur at *a time of change* or *when change is long overdue*. Thus, whenever we meet the dark man at the threshold to the Underworld, we can be sure that we have arrived at some sort of **crossroads; that something is dreadfully wrong in our world;** or that we have taken the first step towards **following desire**.

Crossroads
As we saw in chapter 2, the dark man is associated with *paths* and *roads* of all kinds, but especially with forks, crossroads and other places where routes intersect and choices have to be made. He is also associated with the goddess *Hecate*, who is connected to the concept of *fate*, and who was recognised as the patron of travellers, who erected shrines to her at places where paths and roads crossed. Indeed, dark man experiences frequently contain the imagery of, or take place at, a crossroads, intersection, junction or roundabout, while in folktales and fairytales the dark man regularly enters the story at a point where two paths meet. Furthermore, whenever we reach an important turning point in our own life, we often say that we have 'reached a crossroads', by which we mean the direction of our life has changed, or is about to change, in some significant way.

Actually, the categories of *crossroads, something being wrong in our world* and *following desire* are fairly interwoven and are all turning points of a kind. However, the telltale signs that we are at a *crossroads* are the sense of **fate or destiny** that pervades the situation; the **grief** we may feel about the changes taking place; and the fact that, following these changes, **life will never be the same** as it was before. And this holds true whether the changes we face are *involuntary*, such as those that may be forced upon us as a result of aging, accident, injury, illness, redundancy, etc. or whether we have some degree of *choice* regarding the path we take. For example, I truly wept for the life we left behind when my husband, my children and I had to sell our lovely home and move to a different part of the country. Admittedly, we could have done things differently. But the fact of the matter was that some sort of change was inevitable and, whatever path we had chosen, life would never have been the same again.

Whenever we reach a crossroads, dark man occurrences abound and in many instances they foreshadow the challenging times ahead. For example, my grandma would often speak of the shocking dark man experience she had when 'the Devil' walked up from her cellar and into the kitchen late one night. It scared her out of her wits. But it also heralded the beginning of a turbulent few years that saw her leave her family home, get married and live through the Second World War while my grandad fought on the lines. Similarly, a month or so before Grandma became ill and died, my mum had a distressing dark man dream in which she found herself in a small, dark, closed-in room that was filled with filth and excrement. And Matthew's roadside encounter with the 'shadow man' presaged his terrible accident.

Furthermore, dark man experiences happen thick and fast when we are caught up in times of significant change. Thus, when we were in the process of selling our home, it was as if 'the shadow of death' hung everywhere: I couldn't leave the house without passing a funeral cortège, or so it seemed; I could seldom enter a room or turn my head without a tall, dark shadow slinking from my line of sight; come night-time it would feel as if someone or something was watching us from the shadows, so I began to make sure that all our curtains were tightly shut and that I avoided looking in any mirrors if I had to get up in the night; and I had so many dark man dreams that I began to dread going to bed. Admittedly, this was a time of huge upheaval, which probably goes some way to explaining the sheer number of dark man occurrences. But it wasn't a unique experience, for whenever any of us are living through times of change we all, to a greater or lesser degree, find ourselves meeting the dark man.

Yet it is worth noting that when we meet the dark man at a crossroads in our life, the form he takes tends not to be as malevolent, dangerous or diabolical as it can otherwise be. For instance, when 'the Devil' walked out of Grandma's cellar he was a tall, slim, swarthy-skinned man, with dark eyes, slicked-back dark hair and elegant dark clothing. 'A good-looking fella,' Grandma later conceded. However, despite his eye-catching appearance, Grandma just *knew* who he was and she was having no truck with him. Similarly, Mum's dream of the filthy room was upsetting and Matthew's 'shadow man' was disquieting, yet neither can be described as monstrous apparitions. And the same applies to *most* of the dark man experiences I had while moving home. True, many of the encounters were unpleasant, unsettling or even frightening, but I rarely found myself facing a ravenous, diabolical ogre.

Therefore it seems that when we meet the dark man at a crossroads in our life his intention isn't to scare us witless, but to *wake us up* or *switch on our senses* in preparation for the changes and possible crises that lie ahead. Admittedly, it isn't pleasant to think that such things may be waiting for us around the corner, but dark man encounters at least act as a **forewarning** to stay alert and to take care of ourselves (as Matthew did when he was out riding), so we can be prepared for any untoward events and mitigate the circumstances as best we can. Then again, when we are actually caught up in the often unpleasant and protracted process of change, dark man encounters can act as an **admonition** to stay alert for the leg traps and crosscurrents that may lie on our path; a **reminder** to care for ourselves and stay strong; a **reassurance** as to the *inevitability* and possible *necessity* of these difficult times; and, as we shall soon see, our **direction through the darkness**.

I once heard it said, though, that crossroad-type dark man encounters signify 'the looming shadow of impending catastrophe'. And while there is an element of truth in this statement, to me it's a lopsided and extremely pessimistic way of looking at the phenomenon, for while the dark man does herald the way to change, changes don't have to be difficult or dire. What's more, even if things do become dark and demanding, the dark man doesn't just stand and gloat or turn his back. On the contrary, whenever we feel at our most lost, alone and wretched, we may do well to remember that the Lord of the Underworld has eyes that can see in the dark and that he alone knows the way *home*.

When Something is Very Wrong in Our World

As we have seen, the dark man is connected to the fears and limitations we experience within our world, regardless of whether we are consciously aware of these issues or not. For instance, many people are unaware of the cruel and coercive situations they are caught up in, simply because they've been taught to accept these conditions as normal. Others simply get used to things over time. Many take the blame for other people's aberrations onto themselves, thinking that if only they could be 'better' wives, husbands, sons, daughters, employees, etc. then the other person would love them well and treat them right. And although some problems really are elusive and difficult to bring into the light, more often than not people succumb to a kind of *pseudo-unconsciousness* or *selective stupor* whereby they 'bury their heads' or 'turn a blind eye' to the wrongs that surround them in the hope that they won't have to deal with the issues or that they might simply go away. However, problems of this nature seldom 'go away'; instead they tend to compound, becoming bigger and more complex, terrible and intimidating, until they finally begin to impinge upon our very soul. And when this happens we are in real danger of *losing our life* to the problem for we literally begin to haemorrhage life-force, so that, at best, all that remains is a dried-out husk who merely goes through the motions of day-to-day existence, instead of a vitally alive human being who lives every moment of every day.

In fact, stand on any high street, or in any other place where many different people come together, and you will see this phenomenon in action: the dull, hollow, prematurely ancient faces of those living with a blight on their shoulders, in contrast to the pulsing aliveness of those who are relatively free. You can spot the difference at a thousand paces. But actually doing something about the problem is much harder, for the only solution is for the person to *dig down inside themselves* in order to discover their remaining spark of life, value, goodness and hope, and to hold onto this and use it as a torch to guide them back to life. However, as we have just seen, many people are either unable to recognise that they have a problem or unwilling to do anything about the issues that dog their lives. Yet, fortunately, this is where the dark man comes in, for, whether we are aware of our problems or not, **when the circumstances we are caught up in become so coercive that they begin to impinge upon our soul, the dark man will rear up in an attempt to wake us to the situation**. And when faced with Death most people choose life. Thus meeting the dark man is often enough to make us open our eyes, look at our world and reach out for some sort of solution.

However, even with the dark man opening the way, it is seldom easy to face the problems and issues we have –

consciously or unconsciously – allowed to grow to such gargantuan proportions. What's more, the nature of the situation probably means that we've also arrived at a position of potential conflict with a person or persons who, up until now, have occupied a position of power over us. This can be very discouraging and frightening. It is also a *threshold* experience, for the moment our eyes are opened we are faced with *two choices*: we can acquiesce or 'turn a blind eye' to the situation, but, as we have seen, we can only do this for so long before the situation will literally or figuratively kill us; or we can instigate some sort of positive change within our lives. Admittedly, if we do decide to change we may first have to bide our time or plan a course of action. Nonetheless, **the moment we respond to the dark man's appearance with a positive commitment, the cycle of life will grind onwards and the dark man will open the way to the place where 'the jewels glow'.**[2]

Finally, it should also be noted that the dark man we meet at these times is seldom the attractive Lord of the Underworld who entered Grandma's kitchen, or even the fairly neutral manifestations experienced by Mum and Matthew. On the contrary, whenever the circumstances of life begin to threaten our most fundamental self, the dark man tends to take on more urgent forms which can range from the alarming and the upsetting to the most monstrously malevolent creatures our psyche can concoct. It is at times such as these that we may find ourselves being pursued through our dreams by cold-blooded prowlers, muggers, robbers, rapists, murderers, terrorists and other hideous beasts. What's more, these experiences may spill over into our wakeful states of consciousness so that we may find ourselves feeling unduly threatened by the dangers within our world. For example, an otherwise sane friend of mine called Beatrice is thrown into inexplicable states of terror by certain types of news event. Thus she stockpiled vast amounts of food and water when she feared that the 'Millennium Bug' would bring about the end of civilisation. And, following the 2001 terrorist attacks on the Twin Towers, she bought gas masks for everyone in her family and was ready to spend her life savings on a nuclear-bomb shelter for the back garden. Yet, even though Bea flatly refuses to consider what the real source of her anxieties may be, she can at least cope with life and laugh (sort of) at her behaviour. However, occasionally, when life truly begins to press in around us and the dark man rears up in earnest, some people's coping mechanisms quite simply collapse.

Sally,[3] for example, was a young woman who had a number of problems in her life. But when I met her she was an in-patient at a psychiatric hospital because she couldn't handle 'the dark man' who was chasing her through her dreams and whom she would see, while wide awake, entering a room, standing in a corner or walking down a corridor towards her. The man, she said, was tall and thin, with a horrible shadowy face, staring black eyes, oily hair and smart, dark clothing, though sometimes he seemed to be wearing a billowy black 'cloak' around himself. And Sally was adamant that he was 'evil'. I really felt for Sally, but I couldn't say anything, for, professional ethics aside, any explanation that I could have given would have done *nothing* to help her just then. If anything, it would have made things worse. Sally needed medical help. So, along with the other staff, I just tried to help her talk through her problems; made sure she took her medication; restrained her when she tried to pound her head against a wall in the hope that the pain, blood and uncon-sciousness would make the dark man go away; and supported her while an electric current was passed through her brain in the hope that the 'electric shock treatment' (electro-convulsive therapy or ECT) would improve her mental state.

So you see, the dark man is a very real phenomenon that should never be taken lightly. But, this said, it still confounds me the way most of us can be thrown into a state of panic by something that is a fundamental part of our own mind and being, while simultaneously turning a blind eye to the real and present problems, issues and dangers facing us within the world. It's like getting into a lather at the sight of a monstrous shadow while turning our backs on the monster itself. At best such behaviour is extremely short-sighted, and at worst it is tragically insane.

Following Desire

Many of us have been taught that desire is bad and that to desire anything is weak, selfish, wanton or just plain evil. Yet desire is one of the fundamental driving forces behind creation and it is at the hub of the dark man phenomenon.

In fact, desire, or *Desire*, is another old god/law of nature/archetype that, throughout history, has been depicted in countless different ways, including the sun god **Apollo**; romantic heroes and seducers, such as **Lancelot**; attractive anti-heroes, such as **Robin Hood**; the **youngest son** of countless folktales and fairytales; and various associated objects, such as the **pot of gold at the end of the rainbow**. As dark, cold and grim as the dark man is, Desire is the light, bright opposite. And although Desire can be a devastatingly troublesome archetype to deal with, on the whole, we do tend to enjoy the company of this old god and to welcome 'him' (at least, in part) into our lives.[4, 5]

Unfortunately, we aren't able to look closely at Desire here. However, a basic appreciation of his role is essential to understanding the dark man phenomenon. So, very briefly, Desire is the bright light of day, or the heat of passion, within our otherwise humdrum lives. He may burst in on us like an exploding supernova, whereupon we will suddenly find ourselves 'hit by a thunderbolt' of passion and longing, though not necessarily sexual longing, for we may suddenly become infused with a fervour to visit a foreign country, continue our education, ride a motorcycle, etc. Or he may pad in on velvet paws so that we begin to experience a sense of unrest or a softly niggling idea which gradually grows in strength and intensity until it cannot be ignored. Either way, when Desire enters our workaday world we literally become switched on with life, light, vibrancy and direction. And we also find ourselves faced with two *irreconcilable* choices: we can follow Desire to wherever he may lead us, or we can turn our back on our passion and cut it from our heart.

In chapters 5 and 6, we take a closer look at these two choices. But for now we can note that whenever we choose to follow Desire there is only one place he will take us and that is *into the darkness*. Admittedly, it may seem a little paradoxical that this light, bright god of the air should plunge headlong into the dark, cold Underworld. However, on closer inspection it becomes clear that Desire is not all that he seems. For instance, as well as being the glittering god of the sun, Apollo was a chthonian deity with a terribly cruel streak to his nature; while in our own lives, desire can often be experienced as having a darker, more serious or even disturbing underbelly. Even the sun can be seen to fall from the sky and enter the Underworld every evening at sunset, whereupon, the old stories tell us, it dies before being reborn anew the following morning at dawn. And in mystical traditions the passage of the sun through the darkness is said to be the time of the **black sun** when chaos and the destructive forces of the cosmos are unleashed and Death walks abroad.[6]

Thus, whenever 'desire' arrives in our world and we find ourselves having to make a choice between turning our back on our passion or following it into the unknown, we can be *absolutely certain* that we have arrived at the point where light meets dark in the cycle of life and that the dark man is standing in the shadows watching our every move. What's more, the dark man doesn't remain in the shadows for long, for, as anyone who has danced with desire knows, whenever our lives are filled with life, light and direction, it is only ever a matter of time before the darkness arrives. It is the same principle as the midsummer sun obscuring the shadows but then slipping infinitesimally in the sky so that darkness, winter and death can reassert themselves. And it is an instinctual understanding of this principle that causes many people to literally *shy away* from passion, light and joy before the qualities even have a chance to surface in their lives. These people often *fear happiness* for they believe that upheaval, disaster and/or sorrow will follow close on its heels.[7]

Moreover, the form the dark man takes at these times seems to be largely determined by the way in which we approach desire and the threshold. For instance, **if we dither or procrastinate then our dark man experiences will increase in intensity and unpleasantness until we eventually feel compelled to commit ourselves to one choice or another** – whereupon, if we choose to follow desire, the dark man will open the way to where our treasures lie.

Alternatively, we may be *oblivious* to our surroundings and the choices we have before us. This often happens because, like Persephone picking her flowers or Red Riding Hood dawdling on the path, we are so caught up in our surroundings or so absorbed in our delicious daydreams that we fail to realise that we have crossed the boundary into the inhospitable land. It is not that we don't meet the dark man at these times, because we do. It is just that we are so naïve or so wrapped up in our own interests that we fail to appreciate who or what is standing before us on the path. For instance, Red Riding Hood initially thought the wolf was a charming gentleman, or in some versions of the tale a desirable male, yet even when that old wolf was on his best behaviour the telltale signs of his bestial nature (such as his facial hair, elongated canines or waving tail) were there to see. The little maid, however, **simply didn't notice (or chose to ignore) the markers and so ambled without fuss or elaboration into the Underworld... and the dark man let her pass**. Easy meat, you might say.

Finally, if we intentionally choose to take *a leap of faith* and follow desire into the darkness then the chances are that the dark man will rise up before us in one of his more terrible and terrifying forms. There is a certain logic to this, for in such a situation **the dark man can be said to represent the size of the problem we have before us.** For example, if we currently have no money but we passionately desire to become a billionaire, then to achieve our desire the thought forms, behaviour patterns and external situations that are keeping us penniless will have to be 'killed off' and replaced with new, more financially constructive thoughts, behaviours and situations. It sounds easy, doesn't it? And, in fact, this dissolution of the old and discovery of the new is precisely what takes place as we make our way through the darkness. However, actually making such changes can be a massively challenging, frightening and arduous process, for our old way of life really does have to 'die away' so that we, like the sun, can be born anew. So, when we meet the dark man, or Death, under these circumstances, he can be said to embody the sum of all that we must 'die to' if we are to achieve our heart's desire. Therefore, if we can't face the dark man, we really don't have much chance of making it through the darkness.

Indeed, this **initiatory role** is one that the dark man is often said to occupy in myths, folktales, fairy stories, etc. when he appears as a bridge-keeper, door-warden, gate-master or some other foul creature who sets tasks, asks riddles or otherwise challenges 'the seeker'.[8] Thus meeting the dark man in these circumstances can be considered *a rite of passage* which we must overcome before we can continue our journey. However, it is important to realise that *this is seldom a one-time-only* affair, for if we do feel overwhelmed by the dark man, we can always 'chunk down' a little to make our aims more manageable, or we can step back for a moment to gather new resources, such as increased knowledge or support.[9, 10] Moreover, it's also worth pointing out that the size and scariness of the dark man doesn't *always* correlate with the depth of the journey that we actually take, for a lot can happen between setting out and arriving back home.

And lastly, it is also worth pointing out that as we become more aware of, and familiar with, the process of following our desires through the darkness, so the appearance of the dark man can become increasingly neutral or even positive, which I suppose reflects our improved ability to deal with the changes ahead and the obstacles that we may find along the way.

When Facing Death
A fourth kind of 'threshold' experience, which I suppose we should look at, occurs when we are facing, or are about to face, death. In fact, accidents, illnesses and other types of 'health crises' often occur when we are approaching the point in the cycle where light meets dark, and our old way of life and being faces dissolution in the Underworld. Moreover, as we have seen, the sense of fate or destiny that can accompany serious accidents and illnesses, plus the fact that following them our lives may never be the same again, demonstrates that health crises can, and often do, act as *crossroads* experiences in themselves. However, not all 'near death' dark man experiences happen at times of catabolic change, for instance Caitlin met the dark man while she was 'simply' experiencing difficulties during childbirth, and, while her life undoubtedly changed after the birth of her daughter, it was not the type of all-encompassing dissolution which indicates a person has entered the darkness. No, sometimes, as the saying goes, 'shit happens'. And when it does we can suddenly find ourselves facing death, which is after all the ultimate threshold experience, and often at such times people have dark man experiences. Yet, rather than opening the way into the darkness, many people report that, in these situations, **the dark man actually bars their path**. And the reason for this is that, as *very many* people testify, **it simply wasn't 'their time' to die**.

I can confirm this first hand, in fact, for several years ago, while undergoing major surgery, I 'woke up' to find myself in a womb-like black space, and standing before me was a tall, silent, narrow, featureless, blacker-than-black, masculine entity who would not let me pass, and who, I realised, was acting as a 'hitching post' tethering my soul into life. I remember that immediately after the operation, as I was being wheeled back to my bed, the one thought that kept replaying itself over and over in my head was, 'I've just met the ferryman'. In fact, as I mentioned in the introduction, this experience was one of the things that motivated me to research the dark man phenomenon.

A similar story was told to me by a young woman called Kate[11] following her failed suicide attempt. To begin with, Kate remembered taking an overdose and lying down on her bed to die; when, the next she knew, she was in a gleaming white room, lying on what looked like a hospital trolley. Kate sat up on the trolley, wondering where she was, when a tall, dark man came into the room and walked up to her. At this point, Kate began to sob, for she realised that she knew the man from somewhere, though she didn't know where, and she wanted to stay with him so much. However, the man simply smiled at her and shook his head, whereupon Kate half remembers the ambulance crew and the doctors washing out her stomach at the hospital. Afterwards, she knew that her problems hadn't gone away and that they still had to be faced. However, Kate was adamant that she wouldn't try to take her life again as it just wasn't her time to die. Kate also claimed that before the experience she had felt very alone, but now she knew this wasn't the case, and that she had come back because she had something to do, though she couldn't quite bring to mind what this was.

Finally, a 'strange but true' type story, which although not a 'near death' account, as such, still deserves to be looked at in this category. It began when Julie, a young woman in her late teens, decided to walk home from a nightclub late one night, and it wasn't until she came to her senses all alone in the middle of the local park that she realised what a stupid, dangerous thing this was to do. Julie explained that when the realisation hit her she began to panic, her head began to swim and her legs almost gave out. But she then began to pray with all her heart, and as she prayed a stillness came over her, along with the unmistakable sense that a tall, dark, male shadow was standing behind her, which she knew would protect her. Julie then walked the rest of the way home cocooned in a sense of peace and security, and as she walked in through the front door she thanked God and the dark man for their help and promised that she would never be so foolish again.

Yet, of course, not everyone who has a near death dark man experience lives to tell the tale. After all, the idea of the **Grim Reaper** releasing the dead and the dying from their mortal bodies has to come from somewhere. And, as I have said, Grandma had a vivid dark man experience a short time before she died. Yet on the other hand there are so *very many* accounts of people being **refused passage** or being given a **choice** over whether they live or die. So, on the whole, it does seem that in the vast majority of cases, near death encounters are experienced as positive occurrences, with **the dark man holding the injured, ailing or vulnerable person in life.**

While Passing Through

So what has happened so far is that the dark man appeared in our life and, in one way or another, we met the challenge and crossed the threshold into the darkness. In other words, we have left behind the light, linear world of reason and entered the dark, mysterious realm of the archetypal feminine. Regrettably though, despite many 'new age' type promises to the contrary, we seldom simply pick up our heart's desire the moment we step towards it.[12] On the contrary, as we saw in chapter 3, the Underworld has a definite landscape, thus the moment we cross the threshold we necessarily find ourselves in the cold, claustrophobic and/or downright peculiar *inhospitable land*. And it is through this daunting terrain that we now have to make our way.

In chapter 5 we shall look at what happens to us as we make our way through the Underworld, but for now we can say that the imagery of crossing from light into dark is familiar to us all from countless stories, fairytales, films, etc. For instance, Eve bit into an apple and Paradise was lost; Alice followed the White Rabbit down a rabbit hole into Wonderland; the Miller made a bad bargain for which his daughter had to pay; the King and the Queen forgot to invite the Thirteenth Fairy to Sleeping Beauty's christening; Red Riding Hood tarried on the way to Granny's cottage; and Snow White was abandoned in the forest. In each case, these storybook protagonists either carried out, or were unwittingly caught up in, an action which once performed thrust them out of their familiar surroundings and into a strange and inhospitable environment. And so it is with us, for once we have taken the step and crossed the threshold we inevitably find ourselves alone in the darkness with usually *no idea of where we are and little appreciation of where we are heading.*

Now, as we saw in chapter 3, the Underworld is a feminine environment. Therefore, it is a contentious point precisely what role the dark man – or any other masculine entity – has within it. However, broadly speaking, we can divide all the conflicting ideas on this matter into three general groups, which are:

1. *The Dark Man Cannot Enter the Underworld*: This is the view that as the dark man is a masculine entity he cannot enter the feminine domain of the Underworld. Thus his role becomes similar to that of Cerberus or Charon, in that he acts solely as a gatekeeper, preventing the living from entering the Underworld and the dead from departing. However, although this point of view seems *logically* sound, it doesn't sit well with the old myths and stories, which explicitly tell us that, as the Lord of the Underworld, the dark man does have a role to play within the darkness. Nor does it tally with many people's first-

hand experiences, which again suggest that the dark man, in one form or another, is very much a part of the Underworldly landscape.

2. *The Dark Man Appears at Three Specific Points*: According to this view, we meet the dark man at (a) the threshold into the Underworld, (b) in, or near, the absolute centre and (c) at the far gate. This is an *intuitively* appealing point of view which sits well with a number of myths and stories and with many people's personal experiences. It is also congruent with the mystical 'law of three', which, simply put, claims that both opportunities and challenges come in threes.

3. *The Guide through the Underworld*: This is the position that after we enter the Underworld the dark man stays with us as we make our way through the darkness. It is a position that is backed up by many myths and stories, and also, perhaps more tellingly, by people's actual experiences. However, one needs to exercise caution here, for while we certainly do have a guide through the darkness, there are many who understand this to be a feminine, and not a masculine, presence. What's more, even if we accept that the dark man does exercise this role, there is certainly a limit as to how far he can go, with some saying that he can only go as far as the gateway into the verdant oasis; others that he has a role within this blessed paradise; and a few claiming that he is able to enter the absolute centre. Yet even though it is easy to dismiss these more 'penetrative' ideas as patriarchal attempts to impose themselves into what is unquestionably the feminine holy-of-holies, it must also be acknowledged that on a personal level the dark man *is* sometimes found within the absolute centre of the Underworld and that, especially in his role of *the pale man*, he can act as a marker for this point.[13]

I must now leave it to you to decide the degree of involvement you hold the dark man to have within the Underworld. Alternatively, you may wish to suspend your judgement until you have seen the role the dark man takes within your own life. However, this said, there is one thing we can all be *absolutely certain* of, and it is that, as we enter the darkness, when we feel at our most lost, alone and afraid, there is a presence on hand to help us find our way through the strange and inhospitable land. As Clarissa Pinkola Estés observes:

> The tail [of the Handless Maiden] resurrects a knowing about a very old promise; the promise that the descent will nourish even though it is dark, even though one feels one has lost one's way. Even in the midst of not knowing, not seeing, 'wandering blind,' there is a 'Something,' an inordinately present 'Someone' who keeps pace. We go left, it goes left. We go right, it follows close behind, bearing us up, making a way for us.[14]

Therefore, for the sake of argument, I shall take this presence to be the dark man. That is, we shall assume the truth of point (3) above. And we shall follow him as he helps us make our way through the inhospitable land, into the centre of death and home again. It's a long and challenging journey, which takes us through the most mystical point in the Universe – the unicorn's eye – and which involves an examination of one of its most mysterious concepts – the divine marriage. However, please be aware that this depiction is not set in stone. Instead, think of it a composite that has been woven together into a single story with the aim of providing *a working guide* for anyone who may wish to use it. As such, it may not correlate perfectly with any one person's individual experiences or with any particular spiritual or religious model. However, if this is the case for you, then I would simply say take what you can from what follows – after all, this is the broadest of the three interpretations we looked at above – and use it to deepen your own appreciation of the process.

The Inhospitable Land

After crossing the threshold into the Underworld, we necessarily find ourselves entering the region known as *the inhospitable land*. And, as we saw in chapter 3, this area is usually experienced as:

- **a cold, stark environment**, such as a bleak moorland, an arctic tundra, a barren, rocky landscape, or the icy reaches of outer space;
- **a dark, claustrophobic place**, such as a tangled forest, a confused network of roads, streets or passageways, or an underground warren of paths;
- **a regular(ish) world**, whereupon its chthonian nature will only be revealed by the strange events that occur there, as they did in *Wonderland*, or by some element of the world which is not-quite-right, such as the too-bright colours found in *Oz*.

What's more, in dreams and stories the inhospitable land is often perceived as a **strange or faraway region, country or world**. Thus in ancient times it might have been represented as a nearby village or town, while in today's global community it is often symbolized as a distant planet, a neighbouring universe or a parallel dimension.[15]

Moreover, it is extremely important to realise that *what we take into the inhospitable land is what we experience once we are there*. For instance, if we enter with a clear and open heart then the landscape – be it moorland, forest or Wonderland – will open itself up for us, while if we are clouded and corrupted by fear, prejudice, hate, etc. then the land will close in and become darker, heavier and more oppressive. Accordingly, as most of us occupy a space between these two extremes (we are neither saints nor sinners), so the inhospitable land tends to be experienced as darkish and uncomfortable as opposed to downright adverse. Yet, even so, it is far better to enter this environment with our eyes wide open, our wits about us, and (if possible) with a definite aim or desire in mind, rather than by falling into oblivion without even realising that we have slipped. In fact, the worst scenario occurs when a clouded, confused individual stumbles into the darkness, and their negativity and limitations close in around them and rise up as various hardships, obstacles and demons, yet they have no idea where they are, what is happening to them, or what to do about the situation. This is hell indeed. And unfortunately it is a situation that far too many people find themselves caught up in. Yet even in these dreadful circumstances all is not lost, for regardless of how or why we entered, once we are actually in the Underworld the journey ahead is remarkably similar for everyone, in that – saint, sinner, believer, sceptic, magi or fool – we must all negotiate the same terrain, face the same *sort of* challenges and meet the same individuals that exist within it.

The inhospitable land can also be an extremely confusing environment. In part, this is because it is shaped by feelings, attitudes and emotions as opposed to the regular, logical physical laws we are used to. Thereby, when we are in the inhospitable land, we inevitably find that the thought and behaviour patterns that once served us well no longer function and may even be counter-productive. It can seem as if fate is against us. And we can rapidly become confused, isolated, lost and depressed. Even the heat and light of desire can soon be forgotten as we try to make headway through this disconcerting environment, whereupon we will rapidly lose heart and direction and forget why we came here in the first place.

In fact, most people struggle when they first enter the inhospitable land. This may be because they are wandering oblivious and are unaware of the transition that has taken place; they might be afraid of the literal and/or figurative darkness which has suddenly engulfed their lives; or they may simply fail to appreciate the different laws that govern this alternative state of being. Either way, when we first cross the threshold we all tend to put up some sort of resistance by holding onto that which was trusted and familiar or else stubbornly refusing to adapt to the new. Moreover, this is the time when we are most likely to become hopelessly lost as we stumble around in the darkness, taking wrong turn after wrong turn, losing our sense of desire and direction, and becoming increasingly overwhelmed by feelings of loneliness, futility and despair. It's a sickeningly familiar scenario. Yet even in the worst cases this inward-looking misery cannot last forever,[16] as sooner or later – though maybe not until we have reached our lowest point of desolation and despair – we will stop struggling for long enough to realise that help is (and always was) at hand.

And this is when we meet the dark man once again; for although he is rendered invisible by the darkness of our surroundings, **we now become aware of him standing beside us, opening the way before us, and gently but positively guiding us through the tangled confusion of the inhospitable land**. He was there when we crossed the threshold; he knows who we are, why we are here, where we need to be; and, as the Lord of the Underworld, he knows the lay of this land and exactly which path we need to take. As Clarissa Pinkola Estés observed above, in the midst of our 'not knowing', a way is opened up that takes us directly to where we most need to be. However, don't be fooled into thinking that the path will suddenly become easy. On the contrary, with eyes that can see in the dark, the dark man knows precisely what stands between us and our aim, desire or the next phase of our life and **he relentlessly takes us to the blockages and obstacles that stand between us and our goal**.

Certainly, the number and nature of these obstructions varies with every person, every desire and every individual transit of the Underworld. However, in general, our blocks usually take the form of *psychological blockages* (e.g. fears and beliefs), *social obstacles* (e.g. social and familial conditioning, prejudices, education) and/or *physical obstructions* (e.g. money, location, abilities or obstructive persons). And although meeting our limitations, distortions and inadequacies in this way is seldom a pleasant experience, it is *the only way we have* of making our way through this region of the darkness. Also, the process can be fairly protracted, for, like Sisyphus rolling his boulder up the hill, we must stick to the task until it is completed. As Napoleon Hill observed:

> Sometimes it appears there is a hidden guide whose duty is to test people through all sorts of discouraging experiences. Those who pick themselves up after defeat and keep on trying arrive; and the world cries, 'Bravo! I knew you could do it!' The hidden guide lets no one enjoy great achievement without passing the *persistence test*. Those who can't take it simply do not make the grade...Those who can 'take it' are bountifully rewarded for their persistence. They receive, as their compensation, whatever goal they are pursuing.[17]

Yet such hard-hearted behaviour does little to enamour us towards the dark man or to improve his reputation. Indeed, it is from such experiences that the myths, stories and teachings about the cold-hearted and relentless Lord of the Dead, or the demonic and despicable Devil, have taken form. Yet, while some maintain that the implacable Lord of the Dead continues to challenge us throughout our passage through the inhospitable land and that we only escape his hold when we finally stumble exhausted into the sanctuary of the blessed oasis, there are others who understand that for those who stick to the quest a shift will eventually occur, in that they will start to develop a sense of *trust* towards their dark companion until the moment arrives when they *willingly surrender* their destiny to him. When this happens it is an unmistakably tangible experience which cannot be induced or faked in any way whatsoever. It is also the moment of the **divine marriage** when all 'masculine' attributes, such as control and egotism, are finally dropped and we unite with, or surrender to, that which is somehow beyond ourselves. This hugely portentous event is reflected in numerous myths, such as the disrobing of the goddess Inanna when she descended into the Underworld,[18] and in folklore, by rituals such as the newlywed groom carrying his bride over the threshold and into her new home. Indeed, following the moment of the divine marriage, it does feel as if we are being 'carried' or 'supported', for we suddenly begin to move forward at a phenomenal rate – all blocks and obstacles dissolving before us – until we abruptly step out of the darkness and into the sanctuary of the blessed land.

The Unicorn's Eye
According to legend, the pale or silver-white *unicorn* is a wild and dangerous creature which lives under an apple tree, and which can only be approached safely by an innocent maid; while in the language of symbolism the unicorn is said to represent the absence of all egotistical, wilful and intellectual encumbrances, and to thereby correspond to a condition of humility and grace. Thus the unicorn can be said to *accept* or *denote* a state of innocent, 'naked' femininity, which has been stripped bare of all projective masculine qualities.

Similarly, in esoteric tradition *the unicorn's eye* is said to be one of the most mystical, magical and dangerous places in the entire universe. Admittedly, there is some disparity about precisely what form it takes – whether it is a physical location, a moment in time or a state of mind or being[19] – and there is also disagreement as to where the boundaries should be drawn around this holy-of-holies.[20] However, what is agreed upon is that the unicorn's eye must somehow be negotiated by 'the seeker' who will, however, be *changed or broken* as a result of the encounter. And, as alarming as this may sound, the unicorn's eye is something that we must all pass through any number of times during the course of our life.

The unicorn's eye is, in fact, a region of the Underworld that must be crossed or negotiated by anyone wishing to find their way home. In mystical circles, it is often denoted by the symbol ☽·☾,[21] which reflects the idea that the unicorn's eye is actually composed of three distinct phases or states, which in traditional stories and myths are often depicted as an idyllic garden with a dwelling of some sort at its centre,[22] or as a cottage, house or castle with either a kitchen/stove/hearth or a hidden room at its core. Similarly, following the outline of the Underworld developed in chapter 3, the tripartite unicorn's eye can be seen to be composed of the regions identified as (a) the verdant oasis, (b) the centre of death and (c) the path home.[23] However, as we have seen, there is some disagreement as to the extent of the dark man's role within at least some of these states.

The Verdant Oasis: The extent of the dark man's involvement within the verdant oasis basically hinges on where we experience the divine marriage taking place. **If the divine marriage is experienced** *within the inhospitable land,* **then the dark man usually leaves us on the threshold to the verdant oasis.** His leaving us in this way corresponds to the 'withdrawal of the masculine', which is a common occurrence in many traditional tales, whereupon the heroine's father or husband leaves on a journey, travels to war, or simply drops out of the tale. Additionally, the boundary to the verdant oasis is variously seen as the bottom of a hill, a watery moat (e.g. a stream, river or ocean) or as a more solid barrier (e.g. a wall, fence, door, gateway or, frequently, an arch[24]). And following the dark man's withdrawal, when we enter the verdant oasis, we typically experience it as either deserted or as home to a kindly *older woman*, who is sometimes known as the 'good mother' and who is often said to wear emerald-green. Yet, regardless of whether or not there is anyone on hand to meet us, the verdant oasis is always experienced as a place of bounty and tranquillity, where we can find *food* (frequently, an apple, pear or some other seeded fruit) and *rest* (often, against a tree in the centre of the garden, or in a bed, which may be circular in shape and at the centre of the house).

Alternatively, **if we take the position that our time in the inhospitable land is one long, hard slog until, exhausted, bruised and battered, we stumble across the threshold into the verdant oasis, then we will probably find the dark man *within the verdant oasis*, either tending the garden or house**[25] **or lodging within it.**[26] In these circumstances, the dark man may take on a human form or adopt one of his animalistic guises. And although he will now have a relatively composed and humble persona, we may initially see him as frightening, brutish and coarse, with his more graceful and moderate character only emerging later. It is a situation that is familiar to us from a thousand and one romantic tales, in which a lady comes to see past the apparently unrefined behaviour of her male companion. However, don't let the immature fantasy elements found in some of these stories throw you,[27] for what *must* happen in this situation is that the female must surrender herself to the guardian, whereupon she will *eat food from his garden*, or *have intercourse with him*[28] in the garden, in the central room or on the circular bed, and it is at this point that the divine marriage is consummated and the heroine can lie down to rest.[29]

The Centre of Death: After eating the food of the dead or consummating the divine marriage, the 'maiden' will fall into deep sleep, only to awaken some time later to a very different reality, for she is now in the pupil of the unicorn's eye[30] – or the absolute centre of death – which is the dark and dangerous centre of creation from which all things emerge and to which all things must eventually return.

In myth, fairytales and dreams this centre is often represented as a central room (such as a kitchen, a bedroom, a cellar, or a hidden room deep beneath the roots of the central tree), as a clearing (beside the central tree, in the middle of the forest, etc.) or as the top of a hill or tower. In addition, the centre is usually dark. Thus the kitchen windows may be grimy, the cellar may be windowless, and there will almost certainly be no moon in the sky. However, this is not always the case, and pale surroundings or brightly contrasting black and white are also fairly common.

At, or somewhere close to, the middle of this central room, clearing, etc. there will be a table, an oven or a large cooking pot,[31] and standing beside this there will be *the oldest woman,* who will almost certainly be involved in the preparation of food. Traditionally, this woman has been depicted as an old, black-robed and possibly black-hearted witch, stooping over her bubbling cauldron of broth. However, contemporary interpretations are also common. Thus a friend dreamed that a characteristically beautiful but somewhat older *Honor Blackman* (the actress who played Hera in the 1963 film *Jason and the Argonauts*) offered her a strawberry jam sandwich; while another friend dreamed that her own grandmother gave her a burger from a red, black and white burger van that was parked in the middle of a dark wood.

So, after falling asleep in the blessed oasis, the 'maiden'[32] will wake up to these extraordinary and possibly disturbing surroundings, whereupon the oldest woman will almost certainly offer her something to eat. However, what happens next depends upon *the way in which the maiden approaches the crone.* For instance, if she shows fear, arrogance or any wilful disregard towards the old mother, or if she lies or fails to show the mother due respect, then the moment the food touches the maiden's lips she will wake up back in her humdrum world, probably thinking what a peculiar dream she has just had, and she will have to begin the whole process of meeting the dark man, crossing the threshold, negotiating the inhospitable land, and entering the oasis and the centre, again. However, if this happens to you, please don't despair, for this returning, albeit unfulfilled, to the land of the living is a vital part of the process, as we cannot pass through the centre until we are fully prepared to handle what lies on the other side.[33] Moreover, most of us will experience one of these 'false starts', or even very many, as we journey towards the next phase of our life or our heart's desire. Yet, with each subsequent attempt, we take in to the darkness all that we have learned and gained from our previous efforts.[34] So, with every ensuing passage, our journey will be undertaken with a little more wisdom, dignity and grace.

Alternatively, for those who do approach the old mother with the right attitude of respect, willingness, honesty and trust an entirely different outcome will be experienced; for the moment these people put the crone's food to their lips they will drop down *dead* on the spot; whereupon the oldest woman will strip them naked, take out her old wooden-handled knife or a silver sickle and chop the cadaver into pieces,[35] which she will then drop into the pot, patiently stirring and muttering words of power as she does so. Yet, once again, it is important to realise that this traditional imagery can have variations. So, for example, the witch who locked Rapunzel in the tall tower in the centre of the forest used a pair of silver scissors to cut off the maid's hair; the enchantress in Sleeping Beauty used the needle of a spinning wheel to draw the princess' blood; Snow White was given an apple which caused her to fall into a deathlike sleep; Medea dipped Pelias into a cauldron of boiling liquid to restore him to youth; and although there is no overtly cannibalistic imagery in the two dreams mentioned above, the strawberry jam and burgers can now be seen to take on a somewhat grisly symbolism.

Moreover, it is important to realise this is not mere fairytale imagery. On the contrary, these old tales and dreams are actually reflecting the deeply mystical experience of *death within death*, which, like the journey through the Underworld, the divine marriage, etc. literally occurs at some deeper level of mind and/or being. And, like seismic waves rumbling outwards from the epicentre of an earthquake, so its effects can be felt within our everyday life.

Indeed, in the next two chapters, we take a look at how these processes can actually affect us, when we consider the dark man phenomenon from the perspective of our own lives. However, for now, it is worth noting that what the oldest woman is actually stirring within her cooking pot is *the soup of creation*. Thus, when she drops the cadaver into the mix, she is, in fact, reintroducing us back into life – we are to be reborn. Not only that, but while she is mixing and muttering, the old mother, who is a representative of Fate, is shaping creation. Therefore, when she drops us back into the mix, she is actually ordering things, or stacking fate, so that the opportunities we require to enter the next phase of our life, or to achieve our heart's desire, will naturally open themselves up for us. In crude terms, *she is granting our wish*. However, wishes usually come at a price, and this reordering of our life inevitably means that some (or occasionally very many) parts of our *past life* no longer fit this new model of creation. Thus we must literally die to the old, outmoded parts of ourselves and our existence. And, as you can imagine, the effects of such changes can be wonderful, incredible, extreme and/or cataclysmic from the point of view of our everyday self – which is one reason we have to be fully prepared to deal with them.

But where does the dark man fit into all this? Well, if truth be told, nowhere really, for even if we accept that the dark man does have a role to play within the verdant oasis (and this is by no means certain, for, as we have seen, it is questionable whether anything masculine can enter the unicorn's eye), there is presumably no place for him within the feminine holy-of-holies that is the centre of death. Yet, this said, personal experience cannot be ignored, and there are a number of accounts within which the dark man, or rather *a pale man*, is seen within the centre, silently watching proceedings. In some cases he is thought to be a 'watcher' or the guardian spirit of the seeker, while in others he is said to be a servant or apprentice to the witch. **So even though the dark man's role within this area is at best passive, he can be seen to act as a marker for the centre of death.**

The Path Home: After dropping down dead in the crone's kitchen and being reintroduced to the soup of life, the successful seeker will wake up back in the verdant oasis. Only this time the garden will be filled with a beautiful, warming, golden light. And standing close by we may see a radiant woman, dressed in sky-blue or silver-white, who may be holding a candle; a wand with some sort of light, such as a star, at the end of it; a branch with blossom attached; a reed; an arrow; a diamond; or a chalice of clear water. The garden will also be teeming with life, and we may see birds (particularly doves and swans), a unicorn or a little white she-donkey. And we will probably find that we are no longer naked, or wearing the tired, tattered clothing that we had on when we first entered the oasis, but that we have been re-clothed in beautiful, possibly sky-blue or silver-white attire.

We will also see a path leading out of the garden. This is *the path home* and it may lie beyond an old gate, bridge or archway, and it might meander across rolling fields or through a wood of beech, birch or rowan trees. The lady or one of the creatures may point us in the direction of this path or act as our guide along the way. But it is an open, easy route, with no obstacles or hindrances to impede us. And, as we move along, we will probably feel our hope and optimism rising, though we may also experience a sense of sadness at leaving the Underworld behind. However, once again, it is important to realise that this archetypal scenario may take on a more personal hue when we experience it in our own dreams, daydreams, etc. For instance, my dream of coming out of the nightclub wearing the silver dress and my friend's dream of walking home through Italy were both examples of 'path home' symbolism.

Therefore, as with all archetypal experiences, the path home appears in our consciousness in a way that is meaningful to us. But in this instance don't expect a dramatic saga of gods, heroes and monsters to unfurl itself before your eyes, for, as the old stories suggest, the path home is almost always experienced as a pleasant but fairly uneventful chapter in the journey. Thus there are few myths surrounding the goddess Hestia; the fairy godmother tends to step into the story, wave her wand, then step out again; even epic tales of high adventure usually wind down at this point, with the journey home being represented as a calming lull in what is otherwise end-to-end action.

But what of the dark man? Well, **the path home is the one region of the Underworld where the dark man is never explicitly experienced.** It is the home of the virgin mother, the divine mother or the godmother, who in myth is represented by goddesses such as Hestia and Vesta, and in fairytales is seen to wave her wand and make dreams come true. Nothing masculine, sullied or impure is allowed to enter this place, and the only reason that we have been granted access is because, after dying in the crone's kitchen, we have been purified or regenerated anew. However, all is not as it seems, for following our consummation of the divine marriage – whether this involved having intercourse with the dark man or eating fruit from the land of the dead – we are now carrying his 'seed' hidden deep within the darkness of our belly. In other words, we are ripe with new life, or *the potential to further creation.* And although some call this 'original sin', others recognise it as a 'gift from the gods', for this germ of new life is what allows us to leave the Underworld and it is what we take with us when we re-enter the land of the living.[36]

The Return

So we make our way along the path home. The light and warmth gradually increase as we progress. And it is easy walking, with no obstacles to impede us, for we left all such things behind a lifetime ago. Until, that is, we arrive at a gateway, which we may perceive as standing beside a tree of blackthorn, elder or yew; as an archway, possibly between two trees; as a wrought metal structure; or as an old wooden door. This is *the far gate*, or the doorway out of the Underworld, and all we have to do is walk through it to re-enter life. Yet, although the gate itself tends to be a fairly unobtrusive structure, crossing this final threshold can prove to be the greatest challenge of all – not least because the dark man, as the guardian of the thresholds, must be faced yet again. However, for those who have come so far, the dark man himself is seldom a problem.[37] What *can* be difficult, though, is leaving him and the Underworld behind.

The Challenge

When we arrive at the far gate, we are refreshed, renewed and pregnant with potential. In other words, we are ripe to give birth or step into our new life, and as such it is only right that we leave behind the land of the dead and re-enter the world of the living. **Yet the far gate is a threshold, this time between darkness and light, and as the dark man is the guardian of the thresholds, we will once again have to meet him as we cross.**

However, this time when we meet the dark man, he will no longer appear to be the loathsome and terrifying demon that we were so afraid of when we entered the darkness. On the contrary, what we see before us now is the magnificent Lord of the Underworld, who is often described as tall, dark, lean, quiet and handsome: this is what happened when Belle saw Beast transformed into a man at the end of *Beauty and the Beast*, and when the bear shed his coat to reveal himself as a handsome prince in *Snow White and Rose Red*. Alternatively, the dark man may now be old, tired, grey, ailing or dying. Yet he is still our 'divine husband'. And when we reach the far gate we may find that we have developed a deep emotional attachment to the dark man, which can make it difficult for us to leave the world of darkness and dreams behind.

Furthermore, after the crone has granted us our heart's desire, and her radiant sister, with a wave of her wand, has suddenly taken us to the brink of our dreams coming true,[38] we may feel apprehensive about stepping out of the shadows and taking our 'gift' into the everyday world. There is nothing standing in our way, for, as we have seen, the gate has been swung wide open to allow the diligent seeker to leave with the blessing of the gods. However, after what might have been years spent struggling in the darkness, it may suddenly seem too daunting to take our precious gift into the light of day. In fact, this trial of courage at the far gate seems to be *one of the greatest challenges facing anyone who travels into the Underworld*. Yet it is vital to realise that there are no old gods now throwing obstacles into our path, but that our own reluctance to step forward is all that is holding us back; and some of the fundamental anxieties, desires and doubts that may lie at the root of our reluctance include:

- *fear of the unfamiliar/unknown*: ironically this was one of the main fears to hold us back when we first approached the Underworld, and here at the exit it can hold us back again;
- *issues of self-worth*: we may have lived without our heart's desire for so long, it can now be difficult to accept it as part of our life;
- *fear of loss*: of our precious gift;
- *fear of ridicule and/or destruction*: of the gift or of ourselves;

- *fear of the paper-thin, eggshell-like fragility of the material world*: after the inherent, eternal reality of the Underworld, the material world can seem perilously flimsy;
- *difficulty accepting the material world as 'real'*: in part this can relate to the material world's perceived fragility, but additionally, after experiencing the deeper, more profound reality of the Underworld, it can also become difficult to attach value to the 'passing joys and sorrows, banalities and noisy obscenities'[39] of the everyday world;
- *feeling daunted by where to begin*: after the close and closed-in Underworld, the material world may now appear to be large, loud and confusing. Also, while we have been 'away' in our state of suspended animation, the world will have probably moved on and things will have changed. Thus it can be difficult to know where and how to step back into the mix;
- *love of the womb-like security provided by the Underworld*: during our time in the Underworld we might have developed a strong sense of attachment to it, the 'three sisters' and the dark man, and we may strongly desire to stay in the darkness.

However, unless we are to become a cosseted moon priestess or priest, whose every physical need is attended to by the temple faithful,[40] then sooner or later we must leave the darkness. After all, the heavens must continue rolling and life must be lived. What's more, if we do try to hang back in the Underworld, then we will end up living a kind of half-life, whereupon our mind remains in the darkness while our body tries to survive in the everyday world. We become stuck between worlds. And this is not the elegant 'foot in both worlds' concept that you might have read about, but a graceless, frustrating and uncomfortable existence that leads to us having nothing and getting nowhere fast.

Yet for those who do finally pass through the far gate and step back into life a wonderful surprise awaits, for on their return they discover that they have brought back a knowledge of the Underworld and an ability to communicate with the entities they met while they were there. They have, thus, developed the ability *to see things from below as well as above*: they can perceive what lies at the roots of actions or events, or they can see *what lies behind*. Therefore, on his or her return, the seeker may listen to a person's pretty words, but if they also see/hear/feel the dark man sitting beside them drumming his fingers, then they know that all is not what it seems. Alternatively, if the way ahead looks stark and barren, but then the good mother dressed in emerald-green shows up and points the way, then they can be sure that sustenance and comfort await.

Happily Ever After

So let us imagine that we have travelled through the Underworld, been granted our heart's desire and passed through the far gate. The next obvious question must be 'What now?'. I mean, the implicit assumption throughout this whole adventure has been that if we diligently stick to our quest, then we will ultimately receive the reward of beginning a whole new chapter in our life or arriving at our heart's desire. But is this really the case? Do we really live 'happily ever after' as the story books suggest? Or will nothing change and will our life just continue in much the same way as before?

Before I answer these questions I just want to make it absolutely clear that whatever we take the Underworld, the dark man and the other old gods to be, the process that has been described here is *a genuine and personally observable experience*. On some level of our being, this passage through 'the Underworld' truly does take place and we see evidence of it in our dreams, imagination, wakeful experiences, etc. It really does happen. And one thing we can be absolutely certain of is that, as we pass through the far gate and re-enter the world of the living, *we will have changed as a person*[41] from who we were when we first entered the darkness. And such changes are bound to have an effect on our everyday life.

A second point worth making is that when we passed through the crone's kitchen we really did die to our old life and were reintroduced into a new soup of things. In other words, the context of our life changed. So, when we emerge, new possibilities and opportunities *that did not exist before* will now present themselves. And, most importantly, amongst this new mix will be the opportunity to arrive at or attain our heart's desire – though, as always, the responsibility for actually making and taking our choices ultimately rests with us.

Therefore, we can say that, yes, on exiting the Underworld life will be different, not least because the chances to arrive at our heart's desire will now present themselves. Thus if we take our chances we will attain our goal, whereupon we will live 'happily ever after'. However, this is not the whole story, for, as we have seen, the cycles of life must keep on rolling. So, while 'happily ever after' is a state of contentment[42] that we may bask in for a time, ultimately, it will necessarily dissolve into a humdrum existence, whereupon the whole process will begin once again.[43] And it is this inevitable fall from contentment to dissatisfaction that lies behind such concepts as *the insatiability of desire, the fall of mankind* and *the wheel of karma*.

Finally, you may ask whether we *always* do in fact arrive at our heart's desire. For instance, what if the desire that propelled us into the darkness was, say, lust for an unattainable celebrity or a yearning for something that is impossible to achieve in the everyday world? Well, first, I would have to say that we should all be *very careful* about the things we choose to label as 'impossible'. After all, sailing over the horizon and the two-minute mile were both considered absolutely impossible not so long ago. Second, it seems that while we often do come by the opportunity to *literally attain* our heart's desire, in some cases, when it would not be possible or 'right'[44] for us to do so, we tend to receive *the content of our desire if not the actual form.* Thus, if love is what you truly desire, then love is what you will find, while if a longing for strength and confidence is what drives you, then strength and confidence will be yours – though maybe not on the arm of the particular luminary you once dreamed of.

So this is what comprises the passage through the Underworld and the dark man's role within it. And regardless of where in heaven or on earth the journey actually takes place, it is without doubt a transit that we all must make, at least several times over, in the course of our life. Yet one question remains unanswered, and it is 'Why does the dark man do what he does?'. But as we have seen, this is a devilish question to answer, partly because it presupposes that the dark man is a conscious, rational entity – and this is something that many people will be unwilling to accept – and partly because in answering it we must leave behind the relatively objective observation and documentation of the dark man phenomenon and adopt a more speculative approach.[45]

Why the Dark Man Does What He Does

I am by no means the first person that has tried to give an explanation of why the dark man[46] does the things that he does. However, although many of these other explanations have been put forward by great thinkers, religious sages and towering administrations, a lot of them are couched in the language of religion and religious devotion – sometimes maudlinly, politically or psychotically so. Still, as you may appreciate, it is all but impossible to give a completely neutral account or explanation of something that is as intertwined with our perceptions of the world as are universal archetypes. Thus some subjectivity or concession to the style of the time is inevitable. However, in what follows please remember that I am no mystic, magi or astrophysicist and that this isn't philosophy – it is allegory and supposition. However, on the positive side, this account does draw heavily on the ideas and testimonies of some remarkable thinkers and spiritual ideologies, and it does aim to give a reasonably balanced account of why a sentient, possibly sapient, dark man may do the things that he does. And, as I have already suggested, such an explanation can be useful as we all need a model of reality to work with. Therefore…

In the beginning all that existed was one entity, which at various times and in different traditions has been known by names such as *God*, *All That Is*, *The Cosmos* or *The One*; while in contemporary terms, it may be easier to imagine this entity as a vast single-celled organism, which is either a conscious being or possessing the rudiments of mindful thought.[47]

In time, this entity separated or divided into two component halves. This is sometimes described as a deliberate act, such as when God created the heaven and the Earth,[48] while in other traditions it seems to be a natural and inevitable occurrence, in the same way that oil and water naturally separate when left to stand. What's more, in most theologies these component parts are variously represented as light, reason, masculinity or mind, and darkness, sensation, femininity or matter.

The two halves are then said to 'unite' in some way. In the old creation myths this is often represented by the imagery of the gods coupling to create hierarchical dynasties or family trees (e.g.

the Heliopolitan theology of ancient Egypt or the Olympian complex of ancient Greece); as the 'seduction' or 'corruption' of light by dark (e.g. Judeo-Christianity or the Corpus Hermeticum); while in Tolkein's fictional creation myth, *The Music of the Ainur*, the demiurges or 'Ainur' are said to meld together the music of creation.[49] Yet the one thing that most traditions do agree on is that light and dark never wholly separate and that their coming together eventually results in life as we know it. What's more, it's the impetus behind this amalgamation that effectively reveals to us the reasons behind the dark man's behaviour. And, according to tradition, these reasons tend to fall into one of three categories.

1. *Necessity*: In these situations there is no choice in the matter. The process might be *natural or 'mechanical'*, in which case it doesn't give us any insight into the motivations of a conscious god; it might be *an automatic or reflex action*, which still doesn't reveal much; or it might be *the result of some impartial or arbitrary act*, such as when the ancient Greek gods Zeus, Poseidon and Hades drew lots to see who would preside over which domain. In this case, it is said that Zeus drew the long straw to become the god of heaven, Poseidon drew the oceans, and that Hades drew the short straw to become the god of the Underworld. It is also claimed that Hades was not particularly pleased at drawing the dark and gloomy Underworld, but that he always remained dutiful towards it and showed the greatest respect to the old goddesses, such as Hecate and the Fates, who lived there. So, if this is the case, it can be said that the dark man sacrificed his life above ground in order to **maintain harmony, further creation and uphold the natural order of things**, or that he does what he does because of **obligation or duty**.

2. *Lust*: In this case darkness is said to seduce or corrupt

light. So here we see the 'sons of God' lying with the daughters of men as mentioned in Genesis 6:1–2; or in the Book of Enoch how God's angels, or 'watchers', saw that the daughters of men were beautiful and how they took them for wives and taught them 'sorcery, incantations, the dividing of roots and trees, signs, astronomy, the motion of the moon', metallurgy and other crafts (Enoch 7 – 8).[50] Alternatively, we hear of the archangel Satan, who, because of his lust for power, was cast to earth where he was chained for 'a thousand years';[51] for 'ever and ever';[52] or, as it says in 2 Peter, 'God spared not the angels that sinned, but cast *them* down to hell, and delivered *them* into chains of darkness, to be reserved unto judgment';[53] or again in Jude, 'And the angels which kept not their first estate, but left their own habitation, he hath reserved in everlasting chains under darkness unto the judgement of the great day.'[54] So here we see an unfavourable portrayal of the dark man, who was said to fall to earth or into the darkness[55] because of his **lust for flesh and/or power over creation**. But please remember that this is just one interpretation, and a particularly patriarchal one at that.

3. *Love*: But what if it was *love* that took light into the darkness? First and foremost, this would have to be a love for the darkness itself, i.e. a love for femininity, sensation and matter, which in most myths, stories and ideologies is represented as *the old goddess*. In basic terms, light and dark were once One, and that which was once One can never truly separate. Thus the dark man is the aspect of light or reason which still yearns for sensation and matter. So it is he who returns to the goddess and it is their union which furthers creation. Incidentally, this is one of the reasons why the dark man is demonised by many patriarchal thinkers, who as a rule prize reason above emotions, sensations and feelings, and who like to think that they have

eradicated all trace of these so-called 'feminine' attributes from their psyches. However, as we have seen, it is impossible to do this, for all human beings are comprised of both light and dark. Thus when the urge for sensation arises – as it inevitably does – these thinkers choose to blame it on 'the Devil' or some other external demon, rather than acknowledging it as a part of themselves.

Anyhow, echoes of the dark man's love for the goddess can also be seen on a more microcosmic level in his relationship with the mortal feminine, which in the vast majority of cases means 'women'.[56] After all, couldn't it be said that God's angels actually *fell in love* with the daughters of men and so 'fell from grace' in order to be with them? This certainly seems to be the case, as described throughout *Enoch*, for example:

"It happened after the sons of men had multiplied in those days, that daughters were born to them, elegant and beautiful.

And when the angels [or 'watchers'], the sons of heaven, beheld them, they became enamoured of them, saying to each other, Come, let us select for ourselves wives from the progeny of men, and let us beget children.

Then their leader Samyaza said to them; I fear that you may perhaps be indisposed to the performance of this enterprise;

And I alone shall suffer for so grievous a crime.

But they answered him and said: We all swear;

And bind ourselves by mutual execrations, that we will not change our intention, but execute our projected undertaking.

Then they swore all together, and all bound themselves by mutual execrations. Their whole number was two hundred, who descended upon Ardis, which is the top of mount Armon."[57]

And again, when God rebukes the angels:

"Wherefore have you forsaken the lofty and holy heaven, which endured forever, and have lain with women; have defiled yourselves with the daughters of men; have taken to yourselves wives; have acted like the sons of the earth, and have begotten impious offspring?

You being spiritual, holy and possessing a life which is eternal, have polluted yourselves with women; have begotten carnal blood; have lusted in the blood of men; and have done as those *who are* flesh and blood do.

These however die and perish.

Therefore have I given them to wives, that they might cohabit with them; that sons might be born to them; and that this might be transacted upon earth.

But you from the beginning were made spiritual, possessing a life which is eternal, and not subject to death forever.

Therefore I made not wives for you, because, being spiritual, your dwelling is in heaven."[58]

So the fallen angels did not just lust and leave, but they took the daughters of men as their *wives*, and stayed with them, and taught them the secret arts of civilisation. In fact, according to *Enoch*, the fallen angels were punished for this as much as they were for their relationships with the women, especially 'Azazyel', who 'taught men to make swords, knives, shields, breastplates, the fabrication of mirrors, and the workmanship of bracelets and ornaments, the use of paint, the beautifying of the eyebrows, *the use of* stones of every valuable and select kind, and all sorts of dyes, so that the world became altered'.[59] Thus the angels weren't merely infatuated with power and sex, but they chose to instruct and advance us all.[60]

Therefore **love for the goddess, for the 'daughters of men', or for the whole of mankind** may be the reason why the dark man meets us on the threshold, stays with us through the darkness and continues to hold us in life. And although this may be an unacceptable concept for some – though certainly not for all – it is worth noting that the people who are most infatuated by power and lust are among those who have the greatest difficulty with the dark man, while those who genuinely live by the concept of love tend to find him a more positive, albeit sometimes terrifying, force in their lives. Yet, ultimately, of course, neither I nor anyone else can give a categorical answer to the question of why the dark man does what he does. It is, once again, something that you have to decide for yourselves.

In this chapter we considered what function, or 'job', the dark man performs, and we saw what happens when we first meet him in early childhood, and again when we meet him at the threshold into the Underworld: when we may be at a crossroads in our life; when something may be terribly wrong in our world; when we may be following desire; or when we are facing death. We then considered the role the dark man performs as we make our way through the darkness and, although it is a contentious point, we saw that he acts as our guide when we are lost, alone and afraid in the Underworld, and that at some point we must 'couple' with him in the *divine marriage*, which subsequently allows us to enter the *Unicorn's Eye* or the absolute centre of 'death'. We also saw that the dark man takes a more subdued role within the centre, and when we meet him again at the far gate we may be reluctant to leave him and/or the Underworld behind. However, we noted that when we finally do make this essential break, we never truly separate from the dark man, the three sisters and the darkness, for we can still see, hear or feel them and we will surely return to them one day.

We then looked at what waits for us on the other side of the Underworld, and we saw that it entails the beginning of a brand new phase in our life or the attainment of our heart's desire. However, it was also noted that, in some circumstances, we may achieve *the content of our desire if not the actual form*, and that *happily ever after* is a transient state that ultimately and necessarily falls back into a humdrum existence so that the whole round can begin once again and the cycles of life can continue.

Finally, we briefly considered what reasons a sentient, sapient dark man might have for doing the things that he does, and we saw that, although it is impossible to second-guess the motivations behind any old god's actions, the consensus of opinion suggests that he might be acting on an automatic or involuntary response, or that he may be motivated by obligation, lust or love.

Chapter 5

Introducing... Us

So there we have it. We have seen who (or what) the dark man might be. We have learned how to recognise him when we meet him in dreams, stories, art, waking experiences, etc. We have looked at him in the wider context of the Underworld and seen what function he performs within it. Then we finally thought about why a sentient/sapient dark man might do the things that he does. And this about sums things up for the dark man himself, for, if we want to take our study further, we must now widen the context even more and look at him from the broader perspective of our own lives. In other words, we have to introduce ourselves into the story to see how the dark man fits into our everyday world.

In these next two chapters we shall do just this. First, we shall look at what we 'should' do whenever the dark man appears, for as I look around I see so many people who are genuinely struggling with the dark man and the darkness. It is almost pandemic. Yet I would love to just walk over to these people and whisper to them that it's not really that difficult. True, it can require a lot of courage and commitment to make it through the darkness, but the treasures they so desperately seek *really are* waiting for them on the other side and, even more than this, there is the priceless reward of a life well lived as opposed to an existence of stupor, confusion, avoidance, fear, running away, unhappiness, loss, loneliness, desperation, isolation and despair. We are not alone. We never have been. And all the help and direction we need are within us right now; we just have to learn how to draw on them. Therefore, as well as simply prescribing what we 'should' do when we meet the dark man, this chapter also offers some advice on how we might tune into, and stay in step with, his uncommon and often confusing reality, so that we may subsequently make it through – or out of – the darkness for ourselves.

Again, though, this is not philosophy. It's just straightforward advice based on a lifetime of observing these entities in action and the way that people interact with them – for good or for bad. Indeed, in the next chapter we leave behind what a person 'should' do, and concentrate on what all too often actually happens and how things can go terribly wrong when people react badly towards the dark man, who is after all among the most challenging and frightening of all the old gods. But first, before we continue, it may be helpful to recall what the dark man's relationship is to us, and to keep this in mind as we make our way through the following chapters.

The Dark Man's Relationship to Us

Whether we take the dark man to be a natural dynamic or 'law of nature', a sentient old god or 'demiurge', or one of the basic elements of mind known as 'universal archetypes', he is, as we have seen, a fundamental building block of our world[1] and as such he is **inseparable from ourselves and our surroundings**.

We become aware of the dark man at an early age. And if this happens before we gain awareness into the violation of personal boundaries and the threat to life, we tend to see him as **a positive, reassuring presence who helps us develop a strong sense of insight and intuition**. However, once we experience threat or danger, the dark man picks up these issues and mirrors them back to us, **showing us where the dangers lie, so we can deal with the problem(s) and move on in our life**. However, as very few of us were taught to work with the dark man in this way, what instead tends to happen is that we identify the dark man with the danger itself, and then spend our lives trying to hide from something which cannot possibly be evaded, while turning a blind eye to the very real dangers that surround us in our world.

Also, in certain life-threatening situations, **the dark man is understood to 'hold' us in life.** In effect, this is an extension of him *showing* us the dangers. Only now the dangers are actually upon us, so there is no real chance of escape, and what little fight we have may be diminishing fast. In other words, we are facing death. And, as folklore tells us, this is the time when we meet the 'Reaper', who takes us into the afterlife or who refuses admission and thus leaves us in life.

Finally, the dark man is fundamentally associated with the concept of 'change', and it has long been recognised that **he appears when change is either imminent or long overdue.** When we meet the dark man at these times, he guides us across the threshold and into the Underworld, where, at some point, we must experience the 'divine marriage', when we surrender our egotistical hold on the situation and willingly place ourselves in the hands of that which is **greater, more far-sighted and more deeply in tune with nature than ourselves.** Moreover, as the divine marriage necessarily entails the dropping of our petty illusions and projections, so we once again see the dark man of our earliest childhood – **our friend, ally, guide and protector** – who is now also our **divine partner,** whom we may be extremely reluctant to leave when the time comes to step back into life.

Therefore, as we progress, do try to keep in mind this image of the dark man as an ally, guide and protector, who alerts us to change and the dangers that surround us and who functions to hold us in life. However, this does *not* mean that we should drop our defences and embrace a ravenous, salivating dark man as our new best friend. On the contrary, there are times to pump up our defences and times to relax, and, as we shall see, the two should never be confused.

What We Should Do When He Arrives

At some point in our lives, we all meet the dark man. So much is inevitable. Yet how we react to him at these times does seem to be affected by whether we are at a time of transition, whether we are chasing desire, whether something is very wrong in our world or whether we are facing death. Moreover, our perceptions of the dark man can also be affected by the way he appears to us: whether in our dreams, through a creative medium such as a painting, novel, drama or song, or whether he steps into our waking consciousness. Yet even though our particular circumstances may vary, dark man encounters are almost always disorientating and sometimes extremely frightening. So here are a few basic guidelines that may help you deal with the situation and ready yourself for what is to come.

1. *Do not bolt*: Or at least try not to bolt *too far*. Admittedly, this advice may not be necessary as your experience might simply be surprising, puzzling or disconcerting, and the dark man himself may be more disquieting than alarming. However, dark man experiences can be truly terrifying. And this is especially true if we have avoided him for some time, or, possibly, if we are about to make a significant change in our life. Remember that when we first meet the dark man he represents the composite of all that we must face in order to make such changes. Therefore, if we can't cope with him now in the relative 'light of day', we stand little chance of making it through the darkness.

   Moreover, if the dark man appears as you are taking your first steps towards desire, then *do not stop*! And if you don't understand why he has appeared then try asking yourself some key questions, such as:

   • What is going on in my life that is not conducive to my well-being (or the well-being of my children, my family, my community, my world)?
   • What is it that I need to change (or what is changing)

about me or my life?

- What is not as it seems?
- What do I really want?
- What do I really *not* want?

But don't expect the answers to these questions to simply pop into your mind like the answers to some general knowledge quiz. On the contrary, these particular answers may have a long way to travel before they arrive in your conscious mind. So muse over the questions for a day or so, and keep an eye on your dreams and daydreams in the meantime, and you may eventually get an inkling as to why the dark man has arrived.

Finally, though this is in direct contrast to 'bolting', please do not become mesmerised by the dark man or glamorise or romanticise him at this time. As surprising as it may seem, this is a common response to meeting him – though more so when we encounter him through the creative arts – and, as we shall see, it is a reaction that usually results in negative consequences.

2. *Observe*: Simply take note of your dark man experience. For instance, what did the dark man look like? When did he appear? How did you react? How did he make you feel? What was happening in your life when he arrived? Keeping a journal is an excellent way of observing, but please keep it loose and informal as you are not aiming for high literature here, but are simply keeping a brief record of your dreams, experiences and day-to-day life, so that patterns and associations can be brought into the light.

A word of caution, however. Try to make sure that you don't elaborate on your experiences, for although the vast majority of dark man encounters are relatively simple and straightforward your consciousness may want to complicate and fancify them to make them correspond with what you think *should* have happened or what you *may like* to have happened. In other words, if you're not careful, you may begin to colour your experiences to make them fit with your beliefs and desires.

Similarly, try not to read too much into the experience, for if the dark man has arrived then the process is already underway, so there is no need to force it. There is a real danger here of trying to impose shape, direction and meaning on something which is already occurring. And there is also a danger of scaring yourself stupid in the process, for your mind may take up the experience, and elaborate and agonise over it, until you've fabricated the most gruesome and heart-rending outcomes your psyche can possibly imagine. Yet, as the process is already underway, there is absolutely no value in torturing yourself in this manner.

However, this said, I do believe that there's nothing to be lost by taking it steady or being a little extra vigilant for a day or two (as Matthew was on his motorbike). I don't know whether certain things are predestined or whether fate can be altered or avoided, but I suspect that if something has to happen it will find its form in one way or another, and I am *absolutely certain* that under no circumstances should fate ever be tempted!

3. *Gather resources*: The dark man heralds change and change is often difficult. Yet we can never really tell beforehand what we will have to go through – or how deep and significant the challenge. Sometimes, what appears to be an easy goal suddenly spirals downwards into the abyss, whereas at other times that which seems impossible simply requires minimal tweaking to bring it to fruition. Thus, whenever the dark man appears, we should ideally begin to prepare for the journey ahead, and this means ensuring that our *basic needs* (and the basic needs of our

loved ones and dependants) are, and will be, met and that our *soul groups* are strong and well supported.

Basic needs are the things that we need to do every day (or thereabouts) to maintain our quality of life. Thus breathing is a basic need, as is maintaining our heartbeat. And although both of these things are automatic they can both be fouled up relatively easily by bad diet, lack of exercise, the taking of certain substances, etc. In contrast, personal hygiene is a need which is almost wholly under the control of our conscious mind, though because of this it's an even easier requirement to compromise. Yet the aim here is to make sure that all our basic needs are satisfied, for whenever they aren't we tend to feel, or be, diminished as a human being. Also, while we are in the darkness we may not have the time or the inclination to think about these things as much as we otherwise would.

Basic Needs		
1. maintain heartbeat	7. communication	13. love
2. maintain breathing	8. personal development	14. sleep
3. nutrition	9. creativity/productivity	15. loss/death
4. elimination	10. maintain environment	16. freedom from anxiety
5. personal hygiene	11. sexuality	17. freedom from pain
6. mobility	12. spirituality	

You may be surprised to see 'death' classified as a fundamental requirement on the list of basic needs, above. However, the prospect, or the reality, of loss and/or death is something that we all have to live with every day. And although most people, quite rightly, choose not to dwell on these issues, at some point in our lives most of us have to face them; therefore, it is best to have at least some resources in place to take care of ourselves if and when we do. And this is even more relevant in the context of our journey through the Underworld, which involves *at its heart* the death of the old prior to the birth of the new.

Yet as well as our basic needs, which are fundamental to our existence as a human being and are relatively common to all, we should also, if possible, strengthen our more personal soul groups. To put it simply, soul groups are the people and things in which we invest our time and energy and which help to give us our identity as an individual person. Or, to put it another way, they are the things that we put our *soul* into, and which act as props or supports for our emotional, psychological and sometimes physical well-being. Thus your relationship, your family and your job may be among your soul groups, as might education, adventuring or friends. Basically, our soul groups are the things we care so much about, or feel so much passion for, that we actually draw sustenance from them. And, as a general rule, the more vital and varied our soul groups, the more strength and security we gain. Hence, when the dark man appears it makes sense to invest some time and effort in sorting and strengthening our soul groups, so that we may draw reassurance and support from them while we are travelling in the darkness.[2]

Some Possible Soul Groups

1. family	5. home	9. hobbies
2. health	6. finance	10. education
3. career	7. religion	11. exploration
4. relationships	8. helping others	12. nature

Finally, while we are on the subject of gathering resources and ordering our life, it is interesting to note that when a person is approaching the end of their life, it is said that 'Death' appears some time beforehand to warn them of their impending demise and to give them the opportunity to put their affairs in order – but they are not allowed to tell anyone about the experience. Folklore? An old wives' tale? Possibly. But it cannot be denied that very many people do seem to get a sense that they are about to pass away and do put their affairs in order before they die. For instance, as we saw in chapter 2, my neighbour's brother 'knew' that he would die during a forthcoming surgical procedure and he sorted through his belongings to make sure that his will, etc. were placed where his sister could find them. In fact, Peter survived the actual operation, but within twenty-four hours he had developed serious internal bleeding and he died about five days later. However, I must once again stress that the appearance of the dark man is seldom a portent of actual physical death. On the contrary, it seems that the dark man's job is to help us to make the crossing into the Underworld, which is something that we must all do very many times during *life*.

4. *Stay flexible*: In part, staying flexible means not 'girding our loins' or literally freezing up whenever the dark man appears. Though, admittedly, it can be difficult not to do this, especially if we are anxious or afraid. Yet, more than this, staying flexible refers to the necessity of keeping an open mind with regard to what may be around the corner – for the truth is that, although we may have a good idea of the direction in which our life is heading, we *never* really know for sure.

So, following a dark man experience, please don't sit around waiting for something terrible to happen. As I said before, this is a form of mental torture. And do remember that although change is almost always challenging, it isn't necessarily bad. On the contrary, change can be light, bright, joyful and exciting. Change can be wonderful. And, who knows, maybe some wonderful change is waiting out there for you!

Yet there is another reason why it may be prudent to maintain a relatively open mind with regard to our future, for it has long been said that we create or shape our own reality by the power of our thoughts. Thus, if we dwell on a particular scenario or outcome, then these very events will be magnetised into our life. Consequently, if we agonise over the idea that the dark man's appearance heralds something terrible, then we will actually be calling terror, stress and pain into our lives; while if we think beautiful, happy thoughts, then even bad karma will be mitigated. Is it true, though? Well, the fact of the matter is that I don't know. However, it is interesting to note that while this hypothesis was once the sole province of mysticism, shamanism and some of the more metaphysical philosophers, nowadays an increasing number of scientists are also claiming that it may be the case.

So, with all this in mind, I recommend that, following a dark man experience, you try to maintain a state of *open-minded optimism*, for, while there is no point torturing yourself and calling down negative scenarios, it seems to me that the idea of trying to coerce nature into delivering perpetual sunshine and lollipops could be equally counter-productive.

5. *Gently begin to move*: At some time or another following a dark man encounter we *must* begin to move. Usually, there is no need to rush into this as the passage through the Underworld isn't a race. But after we have noted the experience, observed what is going on in our life and gathered our resources, the time must come when we step out in a particular direction or begin to follow a particular path. True, we should remain flexible and stay tuned into

our feelings, intuitions and the signs and opportunities that surround us. And we should always be prepared to modify our direction when necessary to keep us in line with these cues. However, being open-minded and 'listening to the whispers' should *never* be used as an excuse for inactivity. On the contrary, we can modify our direction, if and when we need to, and eventually we will arrive, but what we can't do is sit on our lily-white behind and just wait for the universe to deliver its treasures into our lap.

If we are already following desire then this shouldn't be too much of a problem as we will already be moving in a particular direction. However, it is important to remember to *keep going*, as, once the initial enthusiasm wears off and we find ourselves coping with the nitty-gritty, we may begin to get 'cold feet', or we might try to talk ourselves out of continuing, coming up with one excuse after another. On the other hand, if we're not sure where we are heading (and, as I have said, who *really* is?), then we should simply set out in a direction that we feel pulled towards. Initially, this could be something as simple as flower-arranging or IT classes. And many people explore a number of these relatively down-to-earth options when they first set out.

Yet, this said, life isn't always a flower-arranging sort of affair, and if you ever realise that you are caught up in a damaging or dangerous situation, then all I can say is, gather as many resources as possible; find trustworthy, useful and possibly professional help; get ready to assert yourself or, if this would be suicide, get out! Of course, I don't want to oversimplify such things, but if you really are in difficulties then you must seek help and/or do something *positive* and *constructive* yourself. When I was working as a nurse astounded me the number of people who were brought into hospital after attempting to commit suicide, who would then tell me, often over breakfast, that they hadn't really wanted to kill themselves; instead they just wanted something (family, partners, employers, landlord, etc.) to change. These people were actually *surrounded* by help and advice, which they could have accessed at any time. However, they still felt that the only thing they had to bargain with was their life, and sometimes it happened that they lost.

Anyhow, when the dark man appears we must sooner or later begin to move, and the trick here is to start out gently. Be easy on yourself, for you probably aren't too sure where you are heading. Try not to impose too much wilful direction on the situation, but listen to your feelings and intuitions. Watch for any opportunities and signs that may occur. And stay alert to your dreams, daydreams, fantasies and any uncommon waking experiences, for, whether you realise it or not, things have changed and you have entered a strange and testing reality (or a challenging time in your life) and the only way you are going to get out of it intact is if you tune into the support and guidance that is there for you.

Dealing with the Difficulties
Yet all this said, it can still be extremely difficult, disorientating and frightening meeting the dark man and then finding ourselves alone in the darkness where our old ways of thinking and coping just don't seem to work any more. And, rather than serenely responding to the situation by observing, gathering our resources and staying flexible, we may instead feel like running away, or rushing forward, whilst fearing what is happening, what isn't happening, what could happen and what may not happen.

Alternatively, we might try to analyse or plan ourselves out of the 'hole' that we have found ourselves in, only to find that any attempt to rationalise ourselves out of the predicament not only fails but actually make things worse, as we start swinging around like a drunken pendulum: reasoning that we'll do this, then changing our mind to doing that, before thinking that we'll do the other. Like a ball in a pinball machine blindly bouncing off one set of circumstances after another, when we are in the Underworld we cannot think clear and straight, and any supposedly logical decisions that we do make only serve to sink us deeper in the mire.

Finally, a third common response to finding ourselves in the darkness is to hunker down and do absolutely nothing.[3] Thus we might bury our head in the sand while our life gradually dissolves into chaos around us. We might repeatedly talk ourselves out of doing anything that might make a positive contribution to our life. Or we may plan on doing all manner of great things, but then grind to a halt as we agonise over minutiae and irrelevancies, such as whether we should buy a Lamborghini or Ferrari with our would-be riches, when in real life we can't even afford a packet of crisps.

But if you recognise yourself in any of these responses, please don't despair, as most of us go through at least some of them every time we enter the darkness. The trick is to catch yourself before you get too lost or too bogged down in your negative behaviour patterns. And thankfully there are a few techniques that can help us do just this.

Mindfulness: Mindfulness is particularly useful when we are frightened, fretting or getting nowhere fast. As described here, it is not a formal meditation technique, but can be likened to the ancient magical practice of drawing a chalk circle around yourself which 'the Devil' cannot enter. Mindfulness simply grounds you in the moment and thus creates a safe space within which you can sit for a while and relax, rebalance yourself, and assess your options, so that you can then move forward with a clearer head and at your own pace.

The best time to practise this technique is when you can sit or stand relatively undisturbed for a few minutes, and it can be especially helpful to incorporate some sort of sensory focus and/or simple practical task into the experience. So sit down with a cup of coffee; if you are on public transport tune into the sounds and sensations around you; do the washing up; sweep the driveway; or while you're in the shower concentrate on the sound and texture of the water. The point of the exercise is simply to focus on what actually *is*, so that your illusions, confusions, anxieties and faraway terrors can be put into perspective. So:

1. Take a deep breath in, close your eyes, and then slowly let your breath out while focussing your attention within your body.
2. Breathe slowly and naturally as you feel, *as if from the inside*, your chest, shoulders, arms, hands, fingers, face, abdomen, back, buttocks, thighs, calves and feet.
3. Open your eyes and slowly look around. Don't force yourself to concentrate on anything, but allow your eyes to move slowly from one thing to another, gently observing its shape, colour, the way it moves, the way the light falls on it, etc.
4. Turn your attention to your other senses. Again, try not to force the issue, but just pause to consider what you can feel (e.g. the breeze on your skin; the texture of the soap bubbles; the weight of the coffee cup in your hand; the way the sweeping brush moves) and what you can hear, smell and taste.
5. Allow yourself the time to appreciate these sensations.
6. Now feel *yourself* within *the surroundings* that you have been observing. Whether you're sitting quietly, washing the dishes, etc. just get a sense of yourself within this environment.

7. You are calm and safe.
8. If you choose, while you are in this state, *briefly and gently* consider any questions that have been bothering you, such as the direction you would like your life to take.
9. Now slowly let your everyday attention return, by maybe giving yourself a little shake, by stretching, or by rubbing and clapping your hands.

You can do this technique in as little as two or three minutes, though five to ten minutes may be optimum, and the grounded, centred feeling it creates should stay with you for some time. Also, the more you practise, the deeper and longer-lasting the effects will be. However, please don't think that you have to become a transcendent being of light to appreciate the benefits of mindfulness. On the contrary, mindfulness is simply a 'rescue' for when your world gets a little out of hand and you just need to stop and pause things for a while.

Breath Focus: Whenever we are afraid our body responds by releasing massive amounts of the chemicals adrenalin and noradrenalin into our bloodstream. It is called the 'fright, fight and flight' response. And it is this response which causes us to stand and defend ourselves or to run away from a dangerous situation. The fright, fight and flight response is 'designed' to save our lives. However, it can go wrong, in that it can prompt us to run away from, or defend ourselves against, the wrong sorts of things, i.e. things which are neutral or even beneficial to our well-being but which we *perceive* as alarming or dangerous. Moreover, the fright, fight and flight response can become a chronic anxiety state (commonly known as 'stress') which destroys our ability to act in the world and which systematically eats away at our mental and physical well-being.

Now, as we have seen, dark man experiences can be very alarming, and even the less frightening occurrences can be worrying or disconcerting. Thus the dark man regularly triggers our fright, fight and flight response even though *he himself* is not a threat but a useful guide. Furthermore, as we are approaching the Underworld and making our way through the darkness, we are often faced with change, demanding choices and trying situations, all of which can throw us into a state of chronic anxiety that actually impedes our ability to think and act, and which eats away at our health and well-being.[4] Thus what we need is a way of temporarily interrupting, and in some cases arresting, our fright, fight and flight response, so that we can steady ourselves, move forward with a little more clarity and poise, and give our mind and body a chance to recover.

There are, in fact, a number of ways in which we can interrupt or calm our stress response – though some are more useful than others. However, one of the easiest and among the most effective is a simple breath control technique whereby we shift from anxious chest breathing to a more relaxed abdominal breathing and maintain this pattern until the stressor has passed or we have relaxed. The reason this technique is effective is that it literally halts one of the major physiological changes triggered by the fright, fight and flight response, which in turn causes the remaining changes to topple like a line of dominoes. Moreover, it's an inconspicuous procedure that can be used almost anywhere, and before or during *any* stressful situation, regardless of whether we are currently caught up in the dark man phenomenon or not. To begin:

1. Shift your attention to your breathing. Just observe how your ribs rise and fall as you breathe in and out.
2. If you are anxious, the chances are that you will be *chest breathing* – your ribs will be moving in and out somewhere in the region of your nipples or armpits, and your breaths will be relatively short and shallow.
3. Gently relax, and shift to a pattern of *abdominal breathing* –

your tummy will rise and fall as you breathe and your breaths will be deeper and probably slower. (It can be especially handy to feel the rise and fall of your tummy against a piece of clothing, such as your waistband; against another part of your body, such as your hand, leg or arm; or against some other object, such as the chair, bed or floor beneath you.)

4. Observe the pattern of your breathing and slow it to a gentle, relaxed rhythm – though not so deep and slow that you begin to go dizzy.

5. Just keep feeling your tummy rise and fall.

Once you have established this pattern of abdominal breathing you can simply keep watching your breaths for as long as you require, and if your mind wanders, simply bring it back as soon as you realise. Alternatively, you can begin to count every out-breath, forwards or backwards, one to ten, repeating the cycle for as long as you need. Or you might add an extra rhythm, such as breathe in... pause for a moment... breathe out... pause for a moment... and so on. Or you could breathe in for a count of four... breathe out to a count of four... breathe in to a count of four... breathe out to a count of four, and keep this pattern going until your mind and body have relaxed.[5]

Journal: As already mentioned, keeping a journal is an excellent way of observing what is going on beneath the surface of your life. As I said, keep it shortish, relaxed and simple – an A5 size diary that you fill in before you go to bed is fine – and use it to make a note of your dreams and any significant events or concerns you may have. The effect of keeping a journal is similar to the 'mindfulness' technique described above, in that what you are doing is becoming a relatively impartial observer of your own life. And as you write, be alert to the *thought and behaviour patterns* that will begin to emerge. For example, if you have a recurring dream, then take a look at what it might signify; if you find yourself repeatedly writing that you are chronically unhappy with a particular situation, then maybe it's time to do something about it; if you keep saying that you 'must' get around to doing something, then this could be a sign that you are procrastinating or avoiding taking the next step in your life; and when the dark man does arrive it can help you to stay balanced and assess your options in a calmer, more insightful and useful way.

Keeping a journal simply foregrounds your desires, concerns, strengths and limitations in a practical, easy way. And it helps you understand a little bit more about who you are, what you are doing and where you want to be.

Just Do It: In the end, though, you can meditate, breathe deeply and write up every scrap of minutiae from your day-to-day life, yet, ultimately, there must come a time when you simply close your eyes, take a deep breath and *get on with the job in hand*. It vexes me no end the number of people who think they can merely send out good vibes, pleasant affirmations, three wishes, etc. in order to have 'the Universe' deliver all of their needs and desires into their outstretched hands.[6] *Grrrr!* Who's going to tell these people that it doesn't work this way and that *personal responsibility* must also feature in the equation?

It's not that I don't believe in the power of intention, because I do. It is just that good intentions *alone* don't pay the bills, feed the children and make dreams come true – it also takes time, effort and often a great deal of hard work. However, this does not mean that we have to live lives of downtrodden misery. On the contrary, we could, and maybe *should*, be having a wonderful time doing the things that we love. Think about it: you've got the time, you've got the tools, and you've got the dark man and all the other old gods in heaven standing behind you showing you the way. This alone must foster some sense of assurance, commitment and courage. So if you are guilty of dragging your feet then just pick up the phone, send off that application, say what has to be said or do whatever else needs to be done in order move on in your life. Get up, get out there and do it!

What We Should Do While Travelling Through

Sooner or later we all end up in the inhospitable land. Whether we deliberately follow desire across the threshold or whether fate catapults us into the darkness, it is inevitable. But the problem then becomes 'What to do?' – for, as we have seen, the inhospitable land is a contrary and potentially hostile environment, within which people can be lost forever (or so it seems), and where the demons of the past must be faced. Moreover, it is while we are making our way through the darkness that we have to negotiate the divine marriage and the unicorn's eye, which can be fearsome obstacles. And this holds true *whatever* we take the dark man and the Underworld to be, and *however* we may rationalise the process.

Yet as daunting, difficult and downright impenetrable as the darkness may seem, there are, once again, some basic guidelines that can help us as we make our way through. As before, they aren't utterly infallible or etched in stone. Instead, they simply provide a little help and direction as we negotiate, or find our way out of, what can be a difficult time of life.

The inhospitable land

1. *Keep moving*: The one thing that we *must* keep in mind is *to keep moving!* The inhospitable land is both literally and figuratively a dark and disorientating place. It is filled with leg traps, false paths and monsters – both the scary and seductive varieties – and, believe me, you will get things wrong in there before you get them right. Yet, if you don't want to become one of the countless lost souls who are living a half-life trapped in the darkness, then you

must keep going. As I said before, we can take all manner of wrong turns, but so long as we learn from our mistakes and keep on moving we *will* eventually arrive.

Another tremendous difficulty with the inhospitable land is its soporific quality: it lulls us into the deepest of sleeps. Thus, while we are making our way through the darkness, it is far too easy to be overcome by lethargy, slumber and beautiful, seductive, empty dreams – which is something we must be ever vigilant against! A prime example of this occurs in the story of the *Little Matchgirl* who, while freezing on a cold winter's night, spends all her remaining energy (her matches) on useless, empty fantasies, before dying under a blanket of snow. And another graphic representation occurs in *The Wizard of Oz*, when Dorothy leaves the yellow-brick road and passes through a field of poppies:

'...they found themselves in the midst of a great meadow of poppies. Now...when there are many of these flowers together their odour is so powerful that anyone who breathes it falls asleep, and if the sleeper is not carried away from the scent of the flowers he sleeps on and on forever. But Dorothy did not know this, nor could she get away from the bright red flowers that were everywhere about; so presently her eyes grew heavy and she felt she must sit down to rest and to sleep...

'If we leave her here she will die,' said the Lion. 'The smell of the flowers is killing us all. I myself can scarcely keep my eyes open and the dog is asleep already.'

It was true; Toto had fallen down beside his little mistress. But the Scarecrow and the Tin Woodman, not being made of flesh, were not troubled by the scent of the flowers.

'Run fast,' said the Scarecrow to the Lion, 'and get out

of this deadly flower-bed as soon as you can. We will bring the little girl with us, but if you should fall asleep you are too big to be carried.'

So the Lion aroused himself and bounded forward as fast as he could go. In a moment he was out of sight.

'Let us make a chair with our hands, and carry her,' said the Scarecrow. So they picked up Toto and put the dog in Dorothy's lap, and then they made a chair with their hands for the seat and their arms for the arms and carried the sleeping girl between them through the flowers.

On and on they walked, and it seemed that the great carpet of deadly flowers that surrounded them would never end. They followed the bend of the river, and at last came upon their friend the Lion, lying fast asleep among the poppies. The flowers had been too strong for the huge beast and he had given up, at last, and fallen only a short distance from the end of the poppy-bed, where the sweet grass spread in beautiful green fields before them.

'We can do nothing for him,' said the Tin Woodman, sadly; 'for he is much too heavy to lift. We must leave him here to sleep on forever, and perhaps he will dream that he has found courage at last.'[7]

'Falling asleep' in the Underworld means succumbing to daydreams and fantasies, maybe about our desire, but possibly concerning any pleasant, distracting fiction. The name for this is *toxic fantasy*, and it serves to sap our creative energy and drain our life-force. It is sheer poison, for instead of being up, moving and following our instincts, if we give in to toxic fantasy we simply lie down and die. The Underworld is quite simply not the place to indulge ourselves with such fancy. As Clarissa Pinkola Estés' Aunt Katerina would say, 'Soft dreams under hard conditions are no good... in tough times we must have tough dreams, real dreams, those that, if we will work diligently and drink our milk to the health of the Virgin, will come true.'[8] And Aunt Katerina was correct.

Yet it's not only daydreams and fantasies that can lull us to sleep in the Underworld, for *toxic behaviour* is just as lethal. Basically, any pastime, action or behaviour that we use to block out the reality of life can have a dulling effect on us, and food, drink, sex, drugs, shopping, TV, etc. are all frequently used in this way.

Therefore when you are in the Underworld stay awake, stay focussed on your desire – even if this is merely the desire for survival – and keep moving towards your desire in whatever way you can. However, what if you wandered into the Underworld without any clear desire or objective? What if you simply woke up to find yourself in this formidable land? Or what if you entered so long ago that you've become lost and isolated in the darkness and have forgotten why you entered or where you are going? You may not even recall the meaning of the words 'desire', 'passion', 'dream' or 'goal'. What then? What is there for you to follow so that you can keep moving?

The answer is that, if you truly cannot find within yourselves even the tiniest spark of desire, then simply *fake it*! You have to move. You have to get the blood flowing again. You have to open your eyes and signal that you are ready for help. Yet be under no illusion; this can take more willpower than you can imagine. But you *have to* begin. And then you have to continue acting 'as if' – as if you know what you want, where you are heading and how you are going to get there.

So, in this situation, simply choose something that feels right, good, positive or just plain okay, and keep on doing it. At first it may feel contrived or false, but in time guidance *will* arrive in the form of inner motivations and outer assistance. Then listen to this guidance, and if it's *honest, positive and forward-looking*, take it up. But please beware that not all so-called 'guidance' is good, and that a lot of shit masquerades under the charade of support in our society. Remember, you are looking towards *grace, goodness and light*, and anything else should be left well alone. Yet, in the meantime, keep moving along the path, following that which feels *right, good and positive*, and when a better idea or offer does arrive (as it will) then grab it with both hands and hold on.

2. *Patterns of behaviour*: I am fascinated by patterns of behaviour. They are the external manifestations of our inner self. They are grounded, mostly, in our subconscious and unconscious thoughts, beliefs and attitudes. And they are visible in the things that we do and say.

Imagine, for instance, that you have a smoke canister attached to you, so that, like an aerial display team, you leave a trail of brightly coloured smoke behind you wherever you go. This trail would eventually outline some of your own patterns of behaviour. And, if you looked at your own smoke trail, would you see yourself going over the same ground day after day, week after week? Would you see yourself repeatedly indulging in toxic behaviour? Or would you see a vital and pulsing web of light in your wake?

Our patterns of behaviour are the manifestation of our place in the world as it is *right now*. They are the representation of who we are and what we believe. And it is often a damned sight easier to look at our patterns of behaviour in order to identify our strengths, hurts, limitations and shortcomings, than it is to undergo hours, weeks and even years of self-indulgent 'anal-ising'. Additionally, patterns of behaviour both *represent* and *shape* our life. Thus, if we want to change anything in our life, we must first change our patterns. It really is that simple.

Now, change can come from the 'inside out'. In other words, if we change our thoughts, beliefs and attitudes then our patterns of behaviour will naturally follow suit. This type of change is typically long lasting, for our mind (especially our subconscious and/or unconscious mind) really does pull the shots. And although it often takes a long, long time to change our beliefs and attitudes, some conversions can happen very quickly. For instance, neuro-linguistic programming (NLP) focuses on changing mindsets in double-quick time. Similarly, many people who undergo an intensely emotional and/or spiritual experience, such as a brush with death, may change their mindset in an instant.

On the other hand, change can come from the 'outside in', and this is what takes place when we begin to act 'as if'. In this case, when we begin to implement new patterns of behaviour, we literally change our place in the world, and so the world *must* change to accommodate this. Affirmations are an example of the outside-in process; another is simply acting the part. For instance, if you want to be rich, then start behaving like a rich person: walk like they walk, speak like they speak, dress like they dress, do what they do (as best you can) and learn to think as they think. It is old magic, but it really does work. But be warned, this is a stirring up technique that will fast-track you to the crone's kitchen. And this is why outside-in procedures can precipitate turbulent times which can take some time to settle.

So if you ever do find yourself in the darkness and you feel like you are stagnating fast, then look to your patterns of behaviour (again, a journal is a good tool to use) and try to alter those patterns so that they are more in line with who/what/where you want to be. Initially, this might mean something as simple as walking on the other side of the road or having brown bread instead of white. But be warned, it can take a lot of determination to stay on track as it is easy to slip back into old routines. Yet, if you do slip, just shake yourself down, pick yourself up and get back on track as soon as possible. Just remember, keep a sharp eye on who/what/where you want to be and *keep moving* towards living that way.

3. *Dealing with the blocks*: Blocks are the things that stand between us and our goal, aim or desire. They can be physical, emotional or psychological. And we all have blocks, otherwise we would already have what we want to have and be who we want to be. Our blocks are the 'monsters' that we find in the Underworld; they are what limit and frighten us; they are the things that stop us moving forward into the life of our dreams. And the whole point of the journey through the darkness is to dissolve or transmute these demons so that we can be/do/have what we desire.[9]

   There are countless books, workshops and individuals that claim to help us overcome our blocks, and very many of them are honest, helpful and true and will surely help you progress – but, again, approach with caution and only surrender your time and money to those which feel right, light and forward-looking. However, there is a time for outside help and a time when you simply have to take a deep breath and get on with the job in hand. And although this is not always easy, sooner or later – while muttering your affirmations, clutching your crystals, twiddling your prayer beads or doing whatever else helps – you must simply 'get up, get out there and do it'. Yet, on a positive note, think of it this way: whenever you reach a barrier you can be *sure* that just beyond it lies the next stage of your life. As Keith Code, the founder of the *California Superbike*

School, says: a barrier is 'anything serving as a limitation or obstruction. A barrier obstructs but is not impassable'.[10] And, 'Whenever you reach [a] barrier you're knocking on the door of your next area to conquer...[a]...barrier is useful because it is telling you that you need to make a few decisions...It is your automatic instructor.[11]

Keith Code is talking about the barriers that motorcycle racers face as they try to lap race circuits in ever faster times. However, much of his remarkably perceptive advice applies equally well to everyday life. For instance, he notes that the signs we have reached a barrier include: making mistakes; feeling helpless or that we 'can't do it'; feeling pressed for time to act; doing nothing, while waiting for something to happen; being unable to get a clear picture of some problem; having our attention stuck on some part of [our life].[12] Again, although these insights are aimed specifically at motorcycle racers, it only takes a small metaphorical leap to see that they are equally relevant to every one of us as we make our way through life.

Finally, how should we deal with our barriers? Well, in short, and once again drawing on Keith Code, we should begin by thinking things through very carefully – by analysing what decisions/actions have brought us to this point, and by gaining a thorough understanding of our problem. Then we should slowly but surely begin experimenting with alternative decisions/actions, *which will inevitably result in different outcomes,* until we either sublimate the monster or break its back. It may come from an unorthodox source, but Keith Code's perceptive advice demonstrates that help can be found in the most unexpected places, and that you don't have to be a super-enlightened being of light to have an excellent grasp on life.

4. *Stay silent*: Some people disagree with this and think that

we should tell everyone we meet about our dreams, hopes and intentions. However, many others believe that there are good reasons for saying *a lot* less. Personally, I think that it is far better to hold the dream inside ourselves, silently allowing it to grow in strength and intensity, until it gains so much power it just *has* to find its expression in the outside world. And by the same token, I find that to talk about our dreams, plans and ambitions – especially when they are at the foetal stage – merely robs them of their power, dissipates their energy and destroys the dream. Even looking at this from a logical point of view, too many people are too willing to dismiss, dislike or deride our dreams and ambitions, so that we need skin like rhino-hide not to feel deflated, discouraged or downright destroyed by their reactions. Therefore keep your plans where they are warm and safe, and where they can grow in strength and intensity, until they are big and tough enough to survive in the outside world.

Alternatively, for a more mystical perspective on the subject, consider what Dr Wayne W. Dyer says about the power of manifestation and 'The Value of Secrecy':

'Making conscious contact with the highest all-creating infinite power is a very private matter. The *naguals* (a Native American term for spiritual masters or sorcerers) and mystics who practice and teach these methods guard their privacy. Moreover, they consider it a violation of their sacred trust to talk to others about their abilities and the 'coincidences' of good fortune.

When we speak to others about our efforts to manifest, our power is weakened. In general, when we describe these activities it is because the ego has entered the picture. This kind of approach considerably dissipates our power of attraction.

It is human nature to talk to others about our problems because we want to alleviate their influence in our life. By sharing, we hope to relieve some of the pressure of the problem. So, too, when we articulate our power to attract something, our attention shifts to the reactions of those in whom we are confiding. Energy is dispersed in the direction of their reactions in the same way that it is when we share problems. The moment a thought is presented to another it is weakened. Maintain privacy concerning your own unique, possibly mysterious to others, powers to attract what you desire. [13']

And, importantly, most people cannot talk and listen at the same time.[14] And I'm not only speaking of the listening that we do with our ears, but also, and perhaps more especially, to the 'listening' that we do in our heart: our feelings, intuitions and instincts. Yet the passage through the Underworld is difficult, and the only way that most of us can make it is if we tune into the help and guidance of something which knows the lay of the land and our reason(s) for being there, i.e. the dark man. However, by chatting to our friends and neighbours we are effectively concentrating our attention on them and the outside world, instead of steadying and silencing ourselves in order to pick up the signals from deep within our own soul. Yet, once again, I leave it to you to decide: stay silent or make your proclamations to the world. You'll have to choose for yourself which approach works best for you.

5. *Protect yourself:* As we have seen, the passage through the Underworld can be hard work, so while you are in the darkness you have to take care of yourself as best you can. First, continue to maintain your basic needs and bolster your soul groups. What's more, remember to take care of the basic needs of those who depend on you, as sometimes,

when people are confused and in the dark, they seem to forget what really matters in life, and, unfortunately, too many people seem to use these circumstances as an excuse for inordinate selfishness.

Second, try not to put yourself into harmful situations. Remember, intuitions and advice can come from various sources, some of which are helpful and some of which aren't. So until you learn to distinguish between the genuinely supportive and the seductively bogus, think things through very carefully. Look towards the consequences of your actions before you act.

Third, take yourself out of negative situations. Again, this isn't an excuse for wanton disregard for others' well-being. However, if you do find yourself caught up in a situation that is draining your life-force and keeping you in the mire then you must take some sort of positive action. Of course, the actions that we take at such times will vary enormously according to our personal circumstances. For instance, we may need to be more assertive, to change our job or to urgently seek professional help. However, as negative situations are a type of 'barrier' to our progress (see above) we should, once again, think things through, think about what choices have brought us to this spot, and then consider what different choices and behaviour might achieve.

Finally, we can once again *stay quiet*. By 'stay quiet' I certainly do not mean 'suffer in silence'. Instead, think of it as quietly going about reordering and getting on with your life without attracting the 'well-meaning' attention of friends and acquaintances. As with the mindfulness technique described above, staying quiet has the effect of drawing a protective circle around ourselves, so that we can stay in touch with our self and our circumstances rather than being distracted and/or bullied by a thousand

and one external offerings. Furthermore, if we are caught up in a certain type of negative situation, then deliberate and calculated silence is essential. Clarissa Pinkola Estés calls this 'backtracking and looping' and explains that it's a technique whereby a hunted animal 'dives under the ground to escape [before popping up] behind the predator's back'. As she says:

'In outer reality, we find women planning their escapes...whether from an old destructive mode, a lover, or a job. She stalls for time, she bides her time, she plans her strategy and calls up her power internally, before she makes an external change.[15]'

You might say that there is no point in calling down the thunder until we're ready to cope with the consequences.

6. **Trust**: Finally, one of the most important things that we can do while we are making our way through dark and difficult times is to *trust*. We have to trust that 'the universe' has an order and balance of which we know next-to-nothing. We have to trust there is a higher power[16] who knows both us and the lay of the land and who can help us through our pain, confusion and misery. And we have to trust ourselves, to believe that we can make it back to the light. No small task, I know. But at some point on the path trust becomes absolutely, inescapably, necessary.

However, please don't be under the illusion that you can sail through all this in a blissful bubble of trust. On the contrary, it can be a long and difficult journey through the darkness. There are times when you will feel lost, alone and confused. You may feel that after every step forward you are knocked back again and again. And 'negative' states such as depression, anger, bargaining, doubt and denial are part of the process. Yet there will also be moments of light, grace and favour, and it is these nuggets of manna that you must hold on to, for it is these that will give you the strength and reassurance to continue.

For instance, in *The Lord of the Rings* Frodo Baggins had crumbs of elven-bread and a small phial of light to help him find his way through the darkness of Mordor. Similarly, I once nursed an elderly priest who was nearing the end of his life. This man had devoted his life to God, but, just an hour or so before he died, he had a crisis of faith. The thought *What if I have been mistaken?* began to plague him. And, in the face of what might be considered the ultimate trial, he lost his trust. Fortunately, one of the other nurses was a devout Christian and she offered to pray with him. So, as the minutes ticked away, the old man and the nurse sat together in prayer until he finally managed to steady himself and find the strength to go forward once more in a state of faith.

I have often wondered what happened to that old priest as he passed away: God, oblivion or something different – how can any of us truly know? However, one thing I *do* know is that prayer, ritual, meditation, kindness, tolerance and love often give us the strength to continue. They help us reconnect to that which is beyond our closed-off everyday world. They allow us to tune in to that which can 'help us through', for they create the space for us to 'listen to the whispers' within our dreams, intuitions, hunches and enthusiasms. On an archetypal level goodness attracts goodness, I suppose. Therefore, the more we open our heart, the more it is filled with grace and favour. Trust begets trust and it lightens the way home.

The Divine Marriage

As we saw in the previous chapter, the divine marriage marks the point in the Underworldly journey when we release our wilful control over the situation and begin to trust in the help and direction of our silent guide. As we noted, however, this is easier said than done, for it *absolutely* cannot be faked. For want of a better term, the divine marriage marks *a shift of soul* rather than a conscious act of will, so in this respect there is little we can do to hasten the process.

However, even if we can't force the divine marriage, there is a great deal we can do to help ourselves arrive at this point. To begin with, we can learn to listen to that which is going on beneath the surface and which usually bubbles up in our insights, intuitions, hunches, dreams and so on. Again, do not simply acquiesce to every hunch you get, for, as we have noted, hunches and intuitions can come from various sources. However, if you do make a point of listening to your deeper feelings you will soon learn to discern those which come from a place of goodness, grace and hope, as opposed to those which originate from a more anxious, limited or even downright tormented source. As a general rule, intuitions and insights which are from a good place feel and sound good, clear and optimistic, and even if what they suggest seems a little scary, it is only so in an empowering and constructive way, while the more negative vibes simply worry us, make us fearful and miserable, and cause our life to contract.

Second, we must learn to *trust* our insights and intuitions, and it is this which involves shifting *some* responsibility away from our logical and wilful mental processes, so that we can instead go with the flow of what we feel within. I say 'some', for I must again stress that personal responsibility entails that we think things through and take account of at least some of the consequences of our actions, for callous, selfish or thoughtless disregard for others' well-being is never, *ever* a part of the higher plan. But when we do learn to relax and take account of the inner whispers, this marks the beginning of the divine marriage, which eventually culminates in our willing surrender to that which is beyond ourselves.

So how do we know that the divine marriage has actually occurred? Well, over the years mystics and other people have attempted to describe this moment of surrender, often in *extremely* abstract, poetic and/or far-fetched terms. Yet, although it can't be denied that inner experiences and feelings such as 'love' or 'peace' are all but impossible to describe in everyday language, and although it seems that many of these people had particularly intense experiences, in more down-to-earth terms, I would simply say that the divine marriage is usually accompanied by a sudden, deep feeling of *acceptance, relaxation and calm,* and a profound sense that everything will, in one way or another, *work out okay* in the end. Admittedly, when it's put like this, it's not grand and it's certainly not sexy. But the divine marriage *is* often marked by a wonderful, deep feeling of all-pervading tranquillity – a post-coital peace. And, ironically, following this moment of unquestioning acceptance, things do begin to move a lot faster than they did before.

The Unicorn's Eye

Following the divine marriage we enter the 'Unicorn's Eye'. The transition is usually fairly swift. And the Unicorn's Eye is, as you may remember, the province of three archetypal personalities: the good mother, the old mother (who is variously represented as the grandmother, the crone, the witch or the wicked stepmother) and the virgin mother (or fairy godmother). Also, up until this moment, the mantra which should have been ringing in your ears is *'keep moving, keep moving, keep moving, keep moving...'*, but now, upon entering the blessed oasis, this will suddenly change to *'rest'*. But note: this is never a slowing down due to despondency or despair; it is simply a need for rest brought about by fatigue. You have been working hard, you have covered a lot of ground, and now you must let go and lie down for a while. You need to sleep.

In fairytales this period of rest is sometimes represented as a deep sleep, a period of confinement, a dark night or a long winter. Yet, importantly, it is seldom a time of inactivity, for massive catabolic changes which transform the life of the central character occur at this time. These changes may take place in the 'inner' world of the protagonist, as they do in *Alice in Wonderland* and *The Wizard of Oz*, or they might occur in the outer world around the resting character, as happens in *Sleeping Beauty* and *Rapunzel*. Similarly, in the everyday world, there are numerous accounts of people who go away for a short break, have a short confining illness, or who undergo some other kind of 'rest', and while they are away their lives are either – by inner transformation or outside occurrences – changed beyond recognition.

But are these changes always for the better? Well, think of the old saying, *'Be careful of what you wish for because it might come true.'* This implies that some changes really aren't desirable. Yet on the other hand, I would say that, although this admonition is worth noting, if you have come so far through the darkness then you're pretty certain to actually *want* what awaits you on the other side of the Underworld. However, this doesn't necessarily mean that the transition will be easy. On the contrary, remember that it is in the Unicorn's Eye that the soup of creation is remixed to incorporate your new way of life, and such a rearranging of energies can be disruptive, unsettling and uncomfortable. So hold on, close your eyes and trust. It's all you can do right now, anyway. But on a positive note, unlike the massively drawn out crises that can throw us into the Underworld, the rearranging of energies in the Unicorn's Eye tends to be, at worst, acute and challenging – 'the shit hitting the fan' is one way of putting it – and, at best, delicious and exciting. Think of *Rapunzel*. In this story the Unicorn's Eye is passed through when Rapunzel kisses the Prince and the old witch finds out about it. In other words, it ain't all bad.

What We Should Do At the Other Side

So you've passed through the Unicorn's Eye, been re-clothed in the garments of your new life, and you're now on the path out of the darkness when you arrive at the far gate. As we have seen, even after all you have been through, this relatively straightforward step can feel like an impossible obstacle as our reluctance to re-enter the light and the world of the living can present the greatest challenge of all. However, as daunting as it seems, it is a step which *must* be taken, and, once again, there are some ways in which we can help ourselves through.

1. *Accept*: After having spent time in the womb-like Underworld, the material world can seem like a harsh, brutal, cruel place. However, it is important to realise that this perception of things is a gross over-simplification, for while some things certainly are cruel and brutal there are also huge swathes of experience that are gentle, nurturing, beautiful, amazing and sublime. The world is wonderful, and, by and large, we see what we want to see within it. Yet this does not mean that we should simply focus on the good bits and pretend that the not-so-good bits don't exist, as this is just as cock-eyed a view as seeing everything as bad. Instead, it's probably best to realise that that which is vital and alive cannot hide in the shadowlands forever: it has its own autonomy; it has to live and express itself. So, basically, all any of us can do is get out there and work with what we've got – the cards in our hand – because that is all that is *ever* available. As Harry Lime said:

   'In Italy for thirty years under the Borgias they had warfare, terror, murder and bloodshed – they produced Michelangelo, Leonardo da Vinci and the Renaissance. In Switzerland they had brotherly love, 500 years of democracy and peace, and what did they produce...? The cuckoo clock.[17']

Now, I am certainly not saying that brutality is good! But what I am saying is that the world is what it is and it's all we ever have to work with, so we might as well stop our griping and grumbling, roll up our sleeves and get on with it. Who knows, if we are true to our heart and work hard enough and long enough, we may even make the world a lighter, brighter place.

2. *Love well*: The perceived impermanence of the physical can make it difficult for some people to step back into the everyday world, for, after spending such a long time in the Underworld, the Underworld can feel strong, solid and enduring, while the material world can seem like a fragile illusion. And this vulnerability can be too much to bear, as the realisation that in a single moment we could lose all that we love and cherish can cripple us and make stepping back into the world a sickeningly difficult choice.

However, as we have seen, life and light cannot – *must not* – remain in the shadowlands forever. Therefore all we can do is recognise that we love the things that we love with all our heart and that we cannot control what happens today, tomorrow or at any other moment in time. It's difficult, I know, but it's our only option if we want to move on in our lives. And one thing that enables us to arrive at this level of grace and magnanimity is *loving well*.

Basically, 'loving well' involves feeling love, expressing love, taking care as best we can, helping to grow and blossom, and giving something of ourselves to those with whom we share a life. On the other hand, loving well *does not* translate into grasping, cringing and cowering in the shadowlands with only our anxieties and complexes for company. Admittedly, loving well is not always easy. But, easy or not, it does seem to be one of our fundamental reasons (if not *the* fundamental reason) for being. As Jack Cornfield observes:

'In the stress and complexity of our lives, we may forget our deepest intentions. But when people come to the end of their life and look back, the questions that they mostly ask are not usually, 'How much is in my bank account?' or 'How many books did I write?' or the like. If you have the privilege of being with a person who is aware at the time of his or her death, you find the questions such a person asks are very simple: 'Did I love well?' 'Did I live fully?' 'Did I learn to let go?'[18]

And again, in the same book he quotes Mother Teresa as saying: 'In this life we cannot do great things. We can only do small things with great love.'[19]

It is also worth pointing out that love is stronger than *anything*. It is the force that makes the world go around. And it can conquer all, even fear, hatred and death. It is said that when the two aeroplanes crashed into the World Trade Center in New York in 2001, the people who were trapped in the burning skyscrapers telephoned their loved ones to express their feelings for one last time: while on the ground ordinary, everyday people performed incredible acts of courage to help those who might possibly escape. So even here, amid the murder, violence, pain and fear, *love found a way*. Similarly, in the days following this atrocity, people risked their lives once again to rescue people's *pets* from the damaged buildings. Thus, in the face of all the grief and terror, the basic goodness and grace of humanity shone through and, as so many times before, *love conquered all*.

3. **Trust**: Again, you must trust. You have come so far and

been through so much, you can trust that you *do* have what it takes to step back into the light. You can trust in the higher power that has helped you get so far and in the underlying harmony of the Universe. And, although nothing is guaranteed, you can trust that the times and tides are with you. Alternatively, if it's love for the dark man, the three sisters and the Underworld that is holding you back (as opposed to a fear of the light), then you must trust that everything you have experienced, learned and gained will stay with you. These things are, after all, a part of who you are, and as you have awoken to their existence they will be with you forever.

4. *Keep moving*: Finally, as before, just *keep moving*. The heavens roll, the planet turns, and we, for our little part, just have to keep going. Life cannot stand still. And although it is true that there are times to rest, to play, or even to dive for cover and hide, the ongoing mantra from birth until death should always be 'keep moving'. It is not a chore, at least not always. It's an adventure in which we should be following our heart – following love – up, down, in, out, around and around in a timeless dance of passion, adoration and tenderness. True, fear and limitation will also be there – at least for the foreseeable future – but please remember that love really does conquer all and that *the dance really does go on*.

Do We Have a Choice?

So there you have it: what a person 'should' do when they meet the dark man and make their way through the Underworld. But this is all well and good until the question 'Do we actually have a choice in all this?' arises. I mean, do we have a choice about whether we meet the dark man or enter the Underworld? And do we have any say in whether we should 'trust', 'love well' or 'keep moving'? If we don't have a choice, then all that remains is the idea that we are little cogs in a big mechanical universe, with no free will or autonomy to call our own. Or else, that this is just another prescriptive doctrine telling people how they *should* live their lives, when, as history has shown us, such directives are notoriously subjective and fallible – at best!

In fact, the answer to the question 'Do we have a choice?' is both 'no' and 'yes'. First, if we consider the idea that intrinsic cycles of life turn, like wheels within wheels, within the whole of creation, then we can see that our life – or rather the rhythm and flow of our life – is to some degree predetermined. However, this is not in conflict with the idea that we have free will, any more than the fact that spring follows summer is a compromise of personal choice. Some things just *are*, and freedom of choice doesn't come in to them. So like the stars and the seasons, the lives of human beings ebb and flow according to an inherent natural rhythm. And periodically dropping into the darkness before rising back to the light is a necessary part of that flow.

Yet, on the other hand, we do have a vast capacity for personal choice *within* these natural limits. For instance, we can choose to live our life in a way that allows us to walk or even run with the flow. Or we can make choices that are detrimental to the free flow of life and which may cause it to falter, distort, stagnate, or even, in extreme cases, reverse! Admittedly, these aberrations cannot last forever and, like a river breaking through a dam, the natural tide will eventually reassert itself. However, the trauma and distress caused by both the disturbance and its self-correction should *in no way* be underestimated. A spontaneous repair and rebalancing can be a devastating occurrence on whatever level it occurs.

Furthermore, I can say that this book *in no way* offers a prescriptive doctrine of how we 'should' live our lives. It is not suggesting that we should conform to one 'correct' model of life (unless, that is, you wish to say that something as general as expressing our self and exploring our life amounts to prescription). But what it does point out is that life follows certain patterns and that within these patterns we are surrounded by an almost infinite array of choices to live our lives in any number of ways. However, as well as offering us a life of wonderful possibilities, such freedom of choice also gives us the chance to really foul things up.[20] Yet it is important to realise that if we do mess things up on an archetypal level then the correction, when it does arrive, is not a matter of vengeful retribution doled out on mortal men and women by some jealous god. On the contrary, it seems that the interruptions and distortions that we create actually effect hideous and cruel contortions *on the old gods*, and that any spontaneous rebalancing only occurs when a sufficient point of tension is reached, causing the archetypal energy to snap itself back. Unfortunately though, as previously mentioned, such snapping back is seldom an easy or comfortable process! However, it can be avoided by simply stopping in our tracks and beginning to heal, and eventually walk with, the old god(s) themselves. And as good a way as any of doing this is to trust, love well, keep moving, etc. But, as ever, the choice is yours.

So in this chapter we widened the context still further to begin looking at the dark man from the even broader perspective of our own lives. We recapped the roles and functions he performs in our lives and looked at how we 'should' approach him when he arrives. We also considered how we can help ourselves get through (or out of) the darkness. However, we also looked at the subject of 'free will' or 'personal choice', and we saw that although the rhythm and flow of life are to some extent fixed, we do have what amounts to an infinite array of choices as to how we express ourselves within these eternal rounds. And, importantly, this means that the advice presented here is just that – advice – and not some inviolable doctrine carved into tablets of unyielding stone.

Chapter 6

When It Goes Wrong

The idea that eternal rhythms or cycles underlie all life and being is certainly not new. As we have already seen, the idea of the circle, or circular cycle, is inherent within many spiritual, metaphysical and philosophical traditions; and the birth-life-death-rebirth cycle of nature, the wheel of karma, reincarnation, astrology and numerology are just some examples of cyclical ideologies. Admittedly, in the various traditions the actual depiction of the circle or cycle can vary somewhat, in that some talk of *circles within circles*[1] that are collectively seen as producing a matrix of balance and harmony. Others use the imagery of *the open circle*,[2] which is often depicted as an ascending stairway, ladder or pathway that is walked around again and again on the way to enlightenment, wholeness, etc. And some use the imagery of *the closed circle*, which is sometimes depicted as a wheel, such as a potter's wheel or cartwheel, upon which we or the phenomenal world are tied, or that of a maze, within which we must journey to the centre. In addition, some traditions combine these ideas, so, for instance, they might talk of a mountain that is home to a pantheon of gods which shape and maintain order within the world

Indeed, the idea of archetypal energies or 'gods' populating, influencing or shaping the cycle of life – and thereby life itself – is, as we have noted, common to just about all times and places.[3] And although the depictions of these old gods vary somewhat as a result of their being 'coloured' by different people's life experiences, one unbroken idea that has woven itself around and around our little planet is that, to preserve the balance and harmony of life, these old gods must be *honoured*.

The idea of 'honouring the gods' has been with us since (at least) the time of the earliest social groups and societies. From vast civilisations, to commanding religious systems, secret societies, mystery schools, small rural communities and everyday people in their homes, all have sought to honour the deities they understood/understand to preside over their lives. Admittedly, today, in our secular, scientific world, many people overtly dismiss the idea of presiding deities and honouring the gods. They argue that such ideas are primitive, foolish or even dangerous. And, in a way, *some* of these people have a point, for a great deal of superstition and confusion does surround the issue, and through the centuries countless acts of downright evil have been perpetrated in its name. Yet, despite all the confusions, contradictions and cock-eyed approaches, the idea that 'old gods' must be honoured remains wholly sound, and is relevant whether you take the gods to be blind laws of nature, conscious, presiding entities or even states of mind. The problem, you see, isn't whether the gods exist, for, as we have seen, in one sense or another they certainly do. No, the problem centres on what constitutes 'honouring', for, as we shall see, many of the things that have been (and still are) done in the name of honour actually have *the exact opposite effect*.

In fact, honouring the gods is a very different practice from what most people assume. It is seldom easy and we frequently – maybe through fear, ignorance, laziness or self-aggrandisement – get it very wrong. However, honouring is a practice that is *essential* to our well-being and the well-being of the people and the planet around us. Therefore, in this chapter, we look at some of the ways in which we fail to honour, and thereby damage our relationship with the dark man, who is, after all, among the most challenging of all the old gods. However, please note that 'honouring', as it is seen here, is not necessarily a 'religious' act, even though people often do approach it from a spiritual standpoint. Nor is it necessary to believe in the old gods as conscious, presiding entities, as the fact of the matter stands if they are blind natural dynamics. In fact, at its heart, 'honouring' simply refers to living *in balance* with our self and our world. Therefore it is a hugely significant concept whatever our outlook on life.

Interrupting the Flow

The dark man is a demanding character. He is seldom experienced as easy or comfortable. And, at worst, he can be inconceivably terrifying. Thus many people have genuine difficulty with this old god, and most people have, at one time or another and in one way or another, run from or 'rejected' him.

Yet on the other hand, some people are so drawn to the dark man and the darkness that they end up leeching off of this old entity, drawing on his energy in an attempt to fuel their own survival or self-image. True, there are times when we should stand side-by-side with the dark man; and there are times when we can lean on him for support; and there are even times when he might step in and carry us until we are able to stand for ourselves. However, these situations are very different from choosing to adhere to or 'violate' him on an ongoing basis.

These two types of distortion – *rejection* and *violation* – are the most common reasons that our relationship with the dark man goes wrong, and we shall presently look at them in more detail. However, there are other attitudes and behaviours that also distort our relationship with this archetypal entity. For instance, we may start to *deify* him, turning him into some idolised divinity,[4] or, in complete contrast, we might *demonise* him and turn him into a pointy-tailed Beelzebub. And both these responses are very common in the world today. Finally, we may simply become *deadened* to the dark man. And again, this is a tragically frequent occurrence.

Yet, as we progress, one thing to bear in mind is that the dark man is simply that – the dark man – and any distortions or chilling experiences that we may have of him necessarily have their roots in *our own* thoughts, beliefs, attitudes and behaviours. *We impose the distortions on the dark man.* Or, to put it another way, *the Devil is in our head and our actions.* Therefore, if and when we do experience a negative projection of the dark man, it is *always* a signal to sort out our own life.

However, one crucial point to make here is that dark man experiences don't just stop at our skin, as it were, for, as we have seen, they can, and often do, refer to the wider circumstances in which we are living. Thus the dark man often has the effect of drawing our attention to the things we are experiencing – on a conscious or unconscious level – within our family, social groups, community, society, environment, culture, etc. Now, I don't want to go into the collective and/or metaphysical dynamics of the dark man experience here, though they certainly do exist. Instead, it is sufficient to say that if and when you have a dark man encounter, don't just sit there contemplating your own navel, but widen your perspective to include your whole life – the people, places and things that surround you, and the personal and collective times you are living through – and your thoughts, attitudes and behaviours towards the whole. So, keeping all this in mind, we shall now look at some of the ways in which we can, and often do, distort our relationship with the dark man.

Rejecting the Dark Man
We reject the dark man whenever we, consciously or otherwise, try to avoid him, or when we try to remain in the world of 'light' as opposed to periodically entering the darkness. And, as the dark man is such a challenging old archetype, such reactions are *very* common. However, common or not, rejecting the dark man inevitably interrupts the flow of life, which necessarily results in disequilibrium or disruption, which in turn manifests as distortion in our thoughts, imagination, behaviour, self-image, perceptions of the world and even in the world itself. And, broadly speaking, there are three different ways in which we can

reject the dark man. We can (a) refuse to approach him, (b) turn and run from him, or (c) try to sidestep him.

a. **Refusing to approach**: Imagine that you know there is something scary down the road. You may know this because a long time ago you went down there and you saw it for yourself. Or perhaps you keep catching glimpses of it from the corner of your eye, or in your dreams. Or maybe people have told you that it is there, that it is terrible, and that you should never go near it. So, as a result, you make a decision to never, *ever* go down that particular path!

   Then again, suppose that you are so comfortable in your little niche that you have no desire to wander far from home. Maybe you are too unimaginative to think that there could be anything else to see or do. Or perhaps you are too busy, too broke, too stressed, too ill, too short, too tall, too young, too old, too male, too female (and so on, and on...) to wander far, even if you wanted to. In this case you'll never go down the road anyway, regardless of what may or may not be waiting around the corner.

   These behaviour patterns can be unconscious, automatic or thoughtless, or they may involve some degree of conscious volition. However, regardless of whether we consciously turn away from the dark man or unconsciously avoid him, the outcome is pretty much the same, in that we stay in the same place, with the same people, having the same conversations, about the same things, in the same life, for years and years on end. Though, if desire ever does manage to wheedle or muscle his way in, then great ambitions and plans *may* be talked about – possibly endlessly and at great depth – but as 'gonna-canna-cudda-wudda-shudda' is a mantra for people who refuse to approach the dark man, nothing much will ever happen.

Except, that is, behind closed doors, closed eyes, or under cover of darkness or the duvet, when people might allow desire to come a little bit closer so that they can experience some of his heat and passion. Yet this is only so they can wallow in *toxic fantasy* and indulge themselves in beautiful, intoxicating dreams of another life, before getting up the next day to find that nothing has changed.[5] Then again, some people refuse to allow desire even this close, and these people are characterised by having no dreams, no passions; they instead think that we should 'make the most of what we've got', 'accept our lot in life', 'stay clean, stay honest and keep our nose to the grindstone'. Anyhow, one way or another, a person who refuses to entertain desire soon becomes a hollow shell, simply going through the motions of life, with nothing to hope for, nothing to aim for, nothing to look forward to (except maybe that noxious fantasy world behind their eyes or their next dose or Prozac) when all they really need to do is to follow the tiniest chink of bright, brilliant sunlight one or two steps too far down the road and into that damned dark forest, whereupon, *with any luck*, they'll meet the terrifying dark man for themselves.

b. *Turning and running*: In this scenario, we are living our everyday life when desire enters and we follow him a little way down the road – until, that is, the dark man appears in front of us, whereupon we drop everything and run back to our everyday life, where, with heart pounding hard and ashen with fear, we *vow* that we'll *never* do anything like that (i.e. anything passionate, risky, different, adventuresome) *ever* again.

Actually, this is an understandable enough first reaction to meeting the dark man. But such a reaction is, or should be, a transient moment that we use to muster our strength, abilities and resources before wholly committing ourselves and setting out again. However, as we just noted, frequently when people meet the dark man they are so spooked that they simply refuse to approach him ever again. 'Once bitten twice shy' tends to be their way of thinking. Yet other people become *infatuation yo-yos*, in that they will be pootling along when an exciting or challenging new opportunity comes to them. They will then pick up this opportunity and run with it for a while, until the times comes to commit themselves to it – i.e. until they feel the dark man approaching – whereupon they'll simply turn heel and run, usually while saying things like, 'Well, I tried, but it didn't work out', 'God doesn't want me to do it', 'It wasn't really my thing, anyway' or 'Hey, baby, hearts can change.' They then go back to their old way of life, only to go through the same behaviour pattern again, and again, and again – until maybe, one day, they grow tired of the yo-yoing and begin to say things like, 'What's the point? No matter what I do and no matter how I try, nothing works out. So I may as well give up trying.' However, when this occurs, they are becoming 'deadened' to the dark man, which is, as we shall see, an even greater cause for concern.

Anyway, this pattern of turning and running can, and frequently does, occur in all manner of different situations. For instance, we might want to further our education but falter on the first day. We may try to change our career, only to fall back at the first hurdle. We may be unable to commit to a long-term relationship. Or we might try new activity after new activity without mastering any of them. And, as with refusing to approach the dark man, turning and running can become a chronic behaviour pattern backed up by reams of specious self-talk.

c. *Trying to sidestep*: We have seen that the dark man guards the threshold between this world and the Underworld, and that when we follow desire (passion/enthusiasm /inspiration) we inevitably step into the darkness and begin a descent of personal growth and change which finally results in the rebirth of a new self or way of being. This is *the path through the unicorn's eye*. And although it can be a long and difficult passage, it is a necessary part of the cycle of life in that it allows and promotes change and growth which is in balance with creation and cosmic harmony.

However, there is a second path we can take that promises to be quicker, less challenging and which does not involve a descent into the forbidding darkness. Sounds good, doesn't it? But this seductively easy way should be avoided at all costs for it is pure poison and it destroys all who walk it. It is sometimes called *the primrose path*, or the path of pleasure and self-indulgence, and, according to Shakespeare, it is the path to hell.

Yet the hell to which the primrose path takes us is not the life-death-life subterranean realm of the dark man and the three sisters. On the contrary, it is a hell of imbalance and gloom which systematically destroys us and our world and which only serves to augment and compound the blocks and monsters that we should be trying to clear. It is a path that causes massive distortion as it completely sidesteps the Underworldly descent and all the time and challenges encountered there. In effect, *the primrose path cuts off an entire half of the natural cycle*, and the damage this causes is immense: it creates a wound that will not stop bleeding and which cannot heal.

So, if we return to the analogy of the road, the primrose path equates to our recognising our desire for some situation or object, but then, knowing that the road ahead is challenging and uncertain, we instead choose to leave the house by the back door... jump over the garden fence...

cross a vegetable patch and several ditches ... squeeze through a hawthorn hedge or three... before arriving back on the road some way beyond where the scary darkness lies. And we may think that we've been extraordinarily clever by taking this 'shortcut'. However, in truth, we have merely created an imbalance, the repercussions of which will spread until they touch all that we hold dear.

In traditional tales, this bypassing of the dark man and the Underworld by taking the primrose path is often portrayed as *wishes* come true. Typically, a wish is a desire that is relatively superficial and which is granted by (a) an inanimate talisman, such as a ring, (b) an entity that is bound to our bidding, such as a genie, or (c) a trickster or some other nefarious being who, under the guise of beneficent helpfulness, willingly and literally grants our every desire. In other words, when we gain the ability to have our wishes come true we gain the ability to shape our destiny (i.e. shape *creation*) from our limited, and usually egotistical, perspective. And this is not only massively unwise, it is actually impossible.

Throughout literary tradition there are examples of how things go disastrously wrong when people gain the power to have their wishes come true. For instance, in Charles Dickens's *The Haunted Man and the Ghost's Bargain* (1848), a man agrees with his doppelganger to have all painful memory removed from his mind, but the result is a hollow shell of a human being. In W.W. Jacobs' *The Monkey's Paw* (1902), a talisman grants an elderly couple three wishes: their first wish is for money, which they get as compensation for their son's death; their second wish is that their son is returned to life, whereupon a rotting carcass drags itself to the door; and their third wish is to save them from the horror that their son has become. (In fact, the *three wishes* motif is among the most common of all fairytale themes, with the first wish, which is usually for money or status, being granted in a literal but tragically unforeseen way, hence the second wish is used to try and put things right but actually only compounds the problem, so the third wish is used to hand things back to nature or fate.) And in Stephen King's *Needful Things* (1991), we see an example of a trickster in the form of shop-owner Leland Gaunt, who arrives in a small rural town and begins to give people what they most desire, whereupon the previously peaceful community descends into pain and chaos.

You see, creation is, as we have observed, maintained by the patient stirring of the old crone's spoon which fashions the flow of nature. And to interrupt or tamper with this flow in our own short-sighted and limited way distorts the flow of the cycle, or warps the balance, which then causes pain and suffering both for us and the world. It is true that we must change and grow as human beings, but we have to work towards our desires (passions/enthusiasms/inspirations) in a way that is compatible with us, our minds, our lives, the lives of those we love, those we share the planet with, and the world itself. This does not mean that other people will always like, or approve of, our choices and actions. But what it does mean is that when we follow desire into the darkness, we are developing, growing and changing as human beings in a way that is compatible or in harmony with Fate, Nature and Being.

The Difference between Wishes and Prayers

The difference between a wish and a prayer is that wishes are self-directed, while prayers implicitly acknowledge that we don't have all the answers and that we need to hand things over to a 'higher' power that does have the foresight and understanding to answer our call in a way that is compatible with life and being – i.e. in grace. Also, when we pray we are invoking the aid of beneficent entities, such as God, Goddess, Angels, Fate, the Cosmos, or the 'higher' aspects of our own unconscious, as opposed to acquiescent, impartial or corrupt entities or talismans.

Yet all this is pretty inconsequential, as wishes are nothing more than a feature of childhood fantasy, aren't they? Well, the answer to this is once again 'yes' and 'no'. It is true that in the literal everyday world genies in lamps, enchanted monkey's paws and good fairies granting our desires with a 'bippity-boppity-boo' are a little thin on the ground, so in this respect, yes, wishes are literary devices. Yet at the same time, we do have plenty of talismans, such as credit cards, which instantly fulfil our wants and desires, and plenty of tricksters, such as high-street shops, ad-men, alcohol, drugs, etc. which promise us the world and then fail to deliver. Therefore it is fair to say that wishes-come-true really are a part of every adult's life! Moreover, even if we ignore credit cards, consumerism and substance abuse, there are plenty of other ways in which we bypass the dark man and take, instead, the primrose path of 'easy' answers. And, as surprising as it may seem, one of the most common ways of avoiding the darkness is by using a certain type of very popular 'productivity technique'.

To understand why this is, we must first remember that the Underworld is the world of darkness, dreams, intuitions and feelings. It is the world of the archetypal feminine, while the everyday world is the masculine reality of logic and light; and, as we have seen, there should be harmony and balance between the two. However, in our modern culture the quality of masculine logic is valued way above feminine intuition, and as a result the feminine has been cheapened and systematically cut out of our lives – especially in traditionally masculine fields such as education and business. Moreover, it is in business that people are most commonly taught, or expected to use, certain techniques that are 'efficient' in that they have the effect of maximizing productivity. Yet the problem here is that these 'productivity techniques' create, perpetuate and compound imbalances, and when used repeatedly they hack deeper and deeper into the natural flow of things, causing ever greater imbalances, which eventually result in an even greater call for increased efficiency and produc-tivity, until one day the system destroys itself... often taking with it everyone and everything it touches. And almost all productivity techniques necessarily involve walking the primrose path.

At their crudest, productivity techniques tend to go something like this: *The 'problem' is the discrepancy between what we now have and what we want to have. So, to solve the problem, we have to effect change. And to effect change we must first consider what we have now, then we should consider what we want to achieve, and then we must logically map a plan of main goals → goals → sub-goals → sub-sub-goals → sub-sub-sub-goals, etc. so that we can trace a daily → weekly → monthly → quarterly → yearly → three-yearly → five-yearly → ten-yearly, etc. plan to where we want to be. Then, we stick like glue to our grand plan. And every minute of every hour of every day, we work towards our goals, ticking them off as we progress.* In these kinds of plans human beings, animals, the environment, happiness (if happiness is even acknowledged!) are reduced to mere statistics. And although the above is something of a caricature, I can assure you that I have sat and listened to quite a few 'successful' business people, who have had plans just like these, and who thought they were doing me a favour in passing on their methods. *Hmmm.*

Anyhow, this does not mean that all goal setting and planning – or credit cards and consumerism for that matter – are bad. On the contrary, if used wisely such things are hugely beneficial and even critically important in our modern society. Besides, we *need* to keep our desires or goals in mind when we are making our way through the darkness, and writing them down is an excellent way of doing this. However, what *is* wrong is thinking that we can plot our path, every step of the way, and then not budge off that path until we have arrived at where we want to be. Instead, what we need as we make our way towards our desires is *intuitive flexibility* which allows us to move and bend according to the particular circumstances we find ourselves in. True, if we bulldoze towards our goal we will probably arrive there a little sooner. But, when we do arrive, we would do well to turn around and look at what we have left in our wake. Those who have passed through the darkness may be a tad more battle scarred, but, on the whole, they will have effected change but not damage as they progressed; while those who have stomped along the primrose path will have probably left a trail of broken relationships, broken promises, broken dreams and lost life, love, happiness and trust behind them. As Brian Mayne, in his book *Goal Mapping*, observes:

'If you are overly strong or egotistical in forcing a goal into existence you may end up creating something that proves to be detrimental or unsustainable in some way, because you will be pushing against the natural flow. If you are too passive and sit back waiting for the goal to happen you may end up waiting a very long time... The key, and balance point, is to *help* your goal happen.[6]'

So we can reject the dark man in a number of different ways. We can refuse to approach him, maybe by getting ourselves stuck in a rut or burying our head in the sand. We can run from him. Or we can attempt to sidestep him, possibly by waving a plastic card, swilling from a bottle or using an aggressive productivity technique. Yet, regardless of how we reject the dark man, the consequences are pretty much the same, in that rejecting him causes **the darkness to become darker and progressively more dangerous, and our perception of him to become increasingly uncompromising and aggressive.** This is the dark man as **predator, aggressor, assailant, marauder.** And he can be a truly terrifying figure.[7]

Violating the Dark Man
We violate the dark man whenever we choose to stay with him and not move on, and this usually happens in one of two places. It can happen when we are in the inhospitable land, in particular when we have just begun to sense his presence as a dark and enigmatic force beside us. And it can happen at the far gate, when it is time to leave the Underworld and the dark man behind.

There are several reasons why we may choose to remain with the dark man at these times. At the far gate, it may be a fear of taking our self, our ideas and/or our creation(s) back into the everyday world, or a genuine attachment to the dark man and the darkness that holds us back. In the inhospitable land, it may be a desire to stay in the fluid darkness of the underground forest, the glamour of 'Underworld work', an egotistical unwillingness to surrender to the dark guide, or it may simply be that we have been struggling for so long that we have forgotten how to let go and trust, even for a short time. However, there is another potentially serious problem that can occur at this time. It is something that is staggeringly common. And it happens when we begin to glorify or romanticise the dark man and then fall head over heals for our creation.

As you may remember, the dark man is never an object of romantic fancy or desire.[8] He is never the chivalrous knight or the dashing hero. And he never takes the role of the suave male lead. Yet when we are down there in the darkness, with the monsters and leg traps biting at us and dragging us down, it is amazing how quickly that strong, dark, enigmatic presence can become an object of passion, and it is astounding how often that passion becomes twisted into an image of self-indulgent, over-sentimentalised fancy. And it isn't just a girl thing either. As they say, 'Women want him, and men want to be him.' Girls and boys both come out to play.

The extent of the problem becomes clearly visible when we look at the thousands of films, songs, stories, etc. that glorify, romanticise and eroticise the dark man/hero/lord. From poems such as Alfred Noyes' *Highwayman* to bodice-ripping Gothic fiction, the romanticised dark man is everywhere. However, the problem with romanticising the dark man is twofold. First, we can be having such a down-in-the-dirt good time indulging ourselves with these fantasies that we actually forget (or choose not to) move on. In other words, they become a toxic substitute for real life. And second, when we bed down with the dark man it drains or 'leeches' the energy out of him, so that the pirates, highwaymen and rebellious rock stars of our fantasies soon become emasculated house-pets or aging vampires that have to drink living blood to survive, and, in this drained state, the dark man loses the energy and the wild sense to lead us anywhere...

to hold us anywhere... to wade in and catch us when we need his help to stay alive.

Thus, when we violate the dark man, he soon ceases to be the master of the wild, dark places, and the print he leaves behind is no longer that of high boot, cloven hoof or wolf's pad. Instead, he becomes **an emasculated wraith** wearing polyester socks and sensible shoes that is trapped within the boundaries of our own neediness for him. And such a situation will be reliably reflected in our dreams, daydreams, etc. where images of **a weak, ineffectual, powerless dark man** will arise. We set up our god and then consumed him.

Deifying and Demonising the Dark Man
The deification and demonising of the dark man are actually types of violation and rejection, but this time with the added element that the dark man is now 'set apart' from us in some way. As you may expect, such distortions are most prevalent in spiritual and religious doctrines, some of which see the dark man as **a celestial divinity**, some of which portray him as **a pointy-tailed diabolus**, and some of which seem to present him as both at the same time. However, on a more down-to-earth scale, those who follow the so-called 'celebrity culture' often project the dark man onto various **well-known people,** who they then either set up as 'gods' or knock back as 'devils'. Additionally, the deifying and demonising of the dark man is often projected onto the phenomenal world, especially in regard to our attitudes towards **material goods and money.**

Whenever we deify the dark man we turn him into some sort of idol, who we see as being separate from ourselves, and whom we stand before and 'worship'. Traditionally, such worship has involved the use of talismans, invocations, prayers, rituals and/or sacrifice, which we may use to show our devotion or respect, to appease the deity, or to beg him/it to reach into our lives and fulfil our needs and wants. So in this case, we have set the dark man 'above' or 'beyond' ourselves, and we then spend our time and energy milling around his feet, looking for *him* to fulfil our needs and desires, instead of looking at our own lives to see what we can do for *ourselves*. Now, I must stress that this is not a slur on religion or spiritual practices, just as it is not a slur on famous people, money or the nice things that we can have in our life. It is simply an observation that people very often place certain icons above or beyond themselves and then sit back to wait for the icon to deliver. And it is this placing above and sitting back that causes the distortion. It is passive and it is often hypocritical. We should be out there in the world *living* our truths instead of merely waiting for God, the universe, celebrities, the economy, etc. to deliver.

Yet on the other hand, the same things that are glorified by some can be perceived as bad or evil by others. So in this case, the dark man is set 'below', as something terrible to be hidden from, avoided or destroyed. Again, talismans, invocations, prayers, rituals and sacrifice are used, only this time to hold him at bay – and as most people feel that it is somehow easier for the demonised dark man to reach into their life than it is the for the deified dark man, they often go to considerable lengths to erect these barriers. Thus, when the dark man is demonised, people do their absolute best to avoid him, which means that they either spend their time doing nothing, or, ironically, taking the primrose path to hell while firmly asserting that if they do any other they will fall into the hands of the demon they fear.

Becoming Deadened to the Dark Man

The final distortion we shall look at occurs when a person becomes 'deadened' to the dark man. It is a terrible thing to happen and unfortunately it is a relatively frequent occurrence. What happens when a person becomes deadened towards anything is that they lose all feeling towards that thing before losing the ability to see it – or to respond to seeing it. In other words, they fall into a kind of 'numb trance' or 'state of waking sleep' which effectively insulates them from the world around them. Deadening usually occurs in response to some physical or emotional trauma. And when it happens suddenly and severely it is an acute medical-psychiatric condition, though such extreme breakdowns are relatively rare. However, it can also occur at a much lower level when it becomes a habitual way of thinking and being. And, unfortunately, this kind of low-key chronic deadening is *very* common.

In relation to the dark man, it is when people are lost in the darkness that they most often become deadened to the dark man. It seems that the continued struggle against the odds causes them to withdraw into themselves. They simply can't see the 'light at the end of the tunnel'. And as they withdraw they become progressively more separated from the deep and knowing instinct that would otherwise see them through. Eventually, there begins to be a hollowness about them – in their eyes, their words, their actions – which suggests that they are simply going through the motions without any real hope or direction. Moreover, as one of the dark man's functions is to hold us in life, so, as a person becomes increasingly deadened to him, they progressively slip out of life: mentally, emotionally and even physically.

The effect of deadening on our dreams, etc. is diverse. We may swing from dreaming about **a ravenous, screaming, tortured dark man** who is maybe trying to jolt us awake, to dreaming about **an ailing, bleeding, dying or even dead dark man** as we weaken. It also seems that waking dark man experiences can become more frequent or apparent at this time, with a number of people citing stories of a dark figure giving them **divine or serendipitous guidance or help**. However, ultimately, it is we, ourselves, who have to dredge up the will to open our eyes and respond to any guidance or help. And although many people manage to do this, many others just can't find it within themselves, and so they continue to live, at best, an empty, hollowed-out half-life within a tragically shrunken existence.

Putting Things Right

As you have probably gathered by now, the dark man is not an easy archetypal energy to live with, and the chances are that you have recognised at least some of your own patterns of behaviour in the descriptions above, for most people have trouble with this old god in at least some areas of their life. Therefore the question now must be, 'How do we put things right?' Or, 'How can we restore the natural balance and flow of things?' And there are several ways in which we can approach this problem.

First, we might look to *natural balance*, or the idea that the universe or nature will somehow correct itself. We have already discussed how nature will only 'allow' things to get so far out of balance before it snaps itself back, usually with devastating consequences, and usually by overcompensating somewhat, like a pendulum wildly swinging from side to side. In fact, at the time of writing the subject of 'boom and bust' economic cycles is very much in the news, while on a wider scale there is a genuine fear among very many people that, because of the havoc we have wrought on the environment, the Earth itself is getting ready to snap back with all the devastation that this would entail. What's more, our own small lives are no different from these bigger systems. Yes, nature will snap them back to restore the balance. However, this is a traumatic process that no sane person would ever want to experience.

Second, is the idea that we might be rescued from our follies and there are two ways of approaching this suggestion. To begin with, there are those who are waiting for *rescue from without*. This may involve the arrival and/or intervention of 'gods', angels, Atlantians, space aliens, channelled beings, elementals, world governments, science, society, our parents, family, friends, neighbours and so on. And it *may* happen. But it may not. Yet even if these individuals or organisations do come to save us, there remains the question of whether we would *want* to be pushed around and moulded like pieces of dough. Moreover, there is also the problem that no external entity could *ever* intervene in our personal relationship with the dark man, as this is something that is within us and deeply bound up with our inner thoughts and feelings. Therefore we could be told what to do; we might even do it; but this would probably just compound the personal imbalances that we experience inside.

Yet there is another angle from which we can approach the idea of rescue, and it is *rescue from within*. According to this view, when things get tough the dark man, or some other 'internal' entity or process, will step in to 'hold us' or 'rescue us' until we get back on the path. It is an idea that we have already considered in this book and there is a great deal of anecdotal evidence to suggest that it really does happen. Admittedly, depending on what stance you take towards the dark man, he may not be viewed as an internal, or a wholly internal, being as such. Yet it cannot be denied that our personal relationship with him is something that takes place deep, deep within ourselves and it is here where the change and rebalancing begins.

Finally, there is the idea that we don't have to wait for things to get outstandingly bad, but that we can stop the flow and turn things around for ourselves. And we can do this *when we choose* and *how we choose*. In other words, we can take personal responsibility for our lives and correct things through our *own volition*. In chapter 5 we saw what we *should* do when the dark man approaches and what we *can do* to get ourselves through the Underworld. And basically, all that we need to do is make the tiniest change in our thought and behaviour patterns and you can be sure that the dark man will arrive to guide us from there. Admittedly, it does take time, effort and commitment to walk this path, for, unlike the shifts imposed by natural balance, these changes don't happen overnight. However, adjustments made this way are gentler and more positive, supportive, holistic and lasting than if we simply waited for nature to correct itself.

In this chapter we returned to the idea of natural cycles and we considered the ancient idea that these cycles are populated, or shaped, by old gods, which must be 'honoured' if the flow and balance of life is to continue. We then considered ways in which human beings can distort or interrupt this flow, and we saw that we can reject, violate, deify, demonise or become deadened to the dark man, and that these behaviour patterns will be reflected in our dark man experiences and, if not corrected, will result in negative, often self-perpetuating, consequences. However, we also saw that such imbalances will not – cannot – remain unchecked, and if they become severe enough nature will eventually 'snap back', with all the devastation that this entails. Rescue from without was another option we considered, though perhaps not a *desirable* option. Then again, we also noted that rescue can also come from within, or that we can simply choose to turn things around for ourselves, and that, although this last alternative usually requires time, effort and commitment, it is by far the most desirable option.

181

Conclusion

Walking with the Dark Man

So here we are at the end of the book, and I hope that what you have read has at least aroused some curiosity within you about your own inner world and the strange and amazing archetypes that move through our psyches and the world around us. As you have probably guessed, though, this is a large subject and all we have been able to do here is scratch its surface. Yet, regardless of how deep we care to look, the dark man remains among the most challenging of all the old gods, and very many people do have genuine difficulty with him. On the other hand, the dark man is also one of the most distinctive and therefore easily recognisable of the old gods. And, perhaps surprisingly, he is also one of the 'easiest' to work with, in that he is fundamentally tied to our everyday life; our dreams, hopes and desires; and also our fears and limitations. Consequently, when you begin to observe the dark man you will be necessarily looking at the limitations and boundaries that you have put around, or *allowed* to be put around, your own life. Though, admittedly, this isn't always a comfortable process.

One of my main aims in writing this book was to open people's eyes to the dark man phenomenon. I *know* it is real because I've been watching these old gods as they have moved through my own and other people's worlds for nearly forty years. I have absolutely *no doubt* that this experience – be it a physical, spiritual or psychic occurrence – happens. And, as I have said, every adult has at least one dark man story to tell, whether this involves a tall, gaunt, swarthy-skinned or skeletal man, dressed in black, stepping into their dreams; strange 'ghost' stories surrounding a similar figure in their waking life; or a dark shadow appearing in front of them and then slipping from view as they turn their head or walk into a room. At the time, many of these experiences are ignored or brushed aside, though some are so shocking that they cannot be dismissed so easily. But with hindsight, it can be seen that many of these incidents happened prior to, or at a time of, change or when change was being actively resisted in the person's life. And this, in a nutshell, is the dark man phenomenon.

In fact, shortly after beginning this book I had a series of my own dark man encounters. The first happened on a Tuesday night when I had a vivid dream that I was riding my bike through rain-sodden streets before turning onto a road that ran beside a huge dark forest. The rain had turned to snow, covering everything in a blanket of white; and I rode through an open gateway, whereupon the road became a rough track that led into the forest, and my bike became a large black horse. I smiled and steeled myself as we galloped into the darkness. I then woke up with a groan, thinking *Oh no, not again!* On the Friday night I had another dream concerning a problem with my bike. Then, on the Sunday, I was riding down a familiar country road on a lovely sunny afternoon when an extremely tall, blacker-than-black shadow appeared among the trees in a small wood just ahead of me. The moment the figure appeared, all the birds that had been roosting in the trees flew up into the air, squawking in alarm and indignation. And I rode on, with a heavy feeling in my stomach and a somewhat heightened sense of awareness. Good job really, because later that day the sunshine unexpectedly turned to rain, and a car pulled out directly in front of me, causing my bike and me to 'hit the road'.

Fortunately, apart from some pretty impressive bruises, I wasn't hurt in the accident, but it did mark the beginning of two-and-a-bit not always easy years of change in which this book had to be shelved on more than one occasion. But, as I have said again and again throughout these pages, I just 'kept on moving', and the fact is that when you do this, and when you keep your ear to the ground so you can pick up the whispers, you *will* eventually make it through.

And so what, after all these years of watching and listening, do I take the dark man to be? Well, when I was young I simply took the archetypes at face value. I thought they were conscious, living entities, whose lives were somehow intertwined with me and my world, and who were somehow more aware of, and involved in, my life than I was in theirs. However, as I grew, and especially after I began to study philosophy, I became aware that these assumptions were just that – assumptions – which simply couldn't be taken at face value. So began the years of searching for answers, at the end of which I had to accept that I just did not, and could not, *know* what these entities were. Admittedly, I have my hunches, but these involve descending deeper into metaphysical philosophy than would be appropriate here, so let's just say that I think that the truth probably (or should that read 'possibly'?) lies somewhere *between* the ideas of a law of nature, an old god and a universal archetype.

The fact is, though, that it is much easier to talk about what the dark man does, as opposed to trying to whittle away at what he is. And, as we have seen, the dark man acts as a way-marker or guide through the turbulence, darkness and fear of change and growth. On a purely biological level, we all go through such changes several times in the course of a lifetime. On an interpersonal level, we will probably go through them several times more. While on a personal level, it seems that we can choose if, how and when we want to grow and develop as human beings, and if we take up this challenge we will meet the dark man again and again. Moreover, it appears that we also go through these cycles of change and development on a *collective level*, which means that as the times and tides change in our societies, cultures and even on a global level, we must periodically enter the darkness *en masse*. Indeed at the time of writing, it seems that the world economy is on the verge of sliding into a phase of darkness. And if it does, we can be sure of several things: (a) dark and confusing times lie ahead, though please remember that not everything in the Underworld is negative, frightening or 'bad', (b) after this period of change, things will be different from what they were before and (c) dark man experiences will come aplenty.

So, again, what is the dark man's relationship to us? Well, as we have seen, the dark man is a fundamental part of us and our world. He was there at the beginning and he will stay with us until the end. However, to begin with, even though the dark man was there, he was totally invisible to us and it was only when our life experiences broadened that he got fleshed out into his recognisable form. There are parallels here with many mythologies and religious stories, not least in the *Garden of Eden* where the serpent resides in Paradise. However, as we have seen, the dark man does not initially take a negative form, and it is only when we become familiar with concepts such as pain, suffering, danger, attack, or the impingement of personal boundaries, that he becomes a more frightening presence. And, again, this parallels the biblical story, for when Adam and Eve acquire knowledge they are cast from Paradise and into the phenomenal world of 'the Devil'.

Finally, it is also worth noting that as well as being a personal experience this colouring of the archetype has a collective dimension. Most obviously this means that people with similar life experiences colour the archetype in a similar way. Thus the ancient Greeks saw Hades, the Romans saw Pluto, and so on. However, there is another suggestion that we are all affected by one another's collective experiences and also, maybe, by the experiences of everyone who has come before. So this means that each of us carries something of the collective history of all humankind, all the goods and bads that have ever occurred, and that this necessarily affect how we see the dark man.

Now, sooner or later, the question of whether all this really matters is bound to arise. I mean, does it matter that we know the dark man? And does it matter whether or not we walk with him? And I suppose that the answer to the first of these questions must be that 'it depends'. After all, I am sure that there are many successful people living rich and fulfilling lives who have no explicit understanding of the dark man phenomenon. However, I would also guess that most of these people have either consciously or unconsciously drawn on a different model of understanding or devised their own ways of dealing with the darkness. You see, it doesn't really matter what we call the dark man or, to a degree, how we rationalise him; instead what really matters is the relationship that we have with him – with ourselves and the world around us – and it is this that makes the difference between a life well lived and mere existence.

It is not about looks, money, status or intrinsic abilities. After all, there are people who possess all these things who are among the most miserable, insecure, unfulfilled people on the planet. And it certainly isn't about poverty and lack, because these aren't exactly recipes for fullness of life and happiness either. No, what is important is our own ability to look into ourselves, to see a better way of being or doing, to face the challenge and step into the unknown, and to slowly and constantly make our way through the darkness as we work towards our tomorrows. It takes strength, courage and determination to do this. It also requires support and assistance. And, as we have seen, it is the dark man who provides us with the orientation, direction and reassurance to make it through the labyrinth. Thus, inasmuch as confusion, fear and limitation need to give way to strength, direction, truth and fulfilment, then, yes, knowing the dark man matters.

And what of 'walking' with the dark man? Well, as we have seen, life and being are composed of natural cycles, some of which we can observe in the way the heavens roll, the seasons pass, the sun rises and falls in the sky, the way that life follows death, and how all our lives are made up of biological, emotional and social cycles. For life and being to exist in harmony, these cycles have to turn – like wheels within wheels – in natural, unbroken precession, and to interrupt them results in distortion, disruption, pain and chaos. Yet as human beings have the capacity *to choose* as well as the inclination *to act* on instinct, so we have the ability to foul things up on a spectacular scale, for ourselves, for others and for the planet. Thus 'walking' with the gods is simply a figurative way of illustrating how we can stay in harmony with the flow and balance of nature. And although there are more old gods in 'heaven' than the dark man alone, he has such a pivotal role and is such a challenging old deity that if we can walk shoulder-to-shoulder with him, even if we don't manage to do this as gracefully as we would like, we will still have taken *a huge step* towards restoring and/or maintaining our natural balance. So walking with the dark man really *does* matter. However, this then invites the question, 'What are we walking towards?'

It's a big question, isn't it – to consider what the ultimate outcome of all this time and effort, of *life itself*, really is? And although it is a subject that has occupied the thoughts of some of the greatest thinkers the world has ever known, it is still a question without a wholly satisfactory answer. For instance, maybe we're simply destined to return to the dust 'from whence we came'. Or then again, we might be caught up in an eternal round of lifetimes, each one following from the last in an endless cosmic merry-go-round. On the other hand, there really might be light at the end of the tunnel, and whether we call this Heaven, Enlightenment, Nirvana, Satori, Oneness, etc. it may truly be attainable and waiting for us to arrive. Maybe, but I don't *know*. Admittedly, I have my suspicions, which, once upon a time, I might have stated bluntly as a matter of fact. But nowadays, I tend to take a more neutral stance towards many things. Personally, I think this makes for a more peaceful way of life as opposed to chasing countless red herrings down innumerable blind alleys and then fighting the point. But ... that's just me.

However, from the perspective of this book I can see two possible outcomes. First, as we walk the round, we may gradually clear all the blocks from the darkness so that only light remains and the dark man is released from his charge of the Underworld. This certainly has parallels with the idea of 'the light at the end of the tunnel', and it may also resonate with those who believe in 'multiple lifetimes' as it would be darn difficult to do all this clearing work in the space of just one life. Yet a second possibility is that the whole point of being here is just to do our best and have as good a time as possible along the way. So, in this case, we should simply enjoy working towards our 'happily ever afters', as fleeting and phenomenal as they may be, for it is through this process that balance and harmony are maintained, and if we can make the most of the journey as well as the desti-nation then so much the better. It is an idea that is congruent with both the single and multiple lifetime(s) point of view, as regardless of whether we, ourselves, are destined to return, we will simply be leaving the world in *at least* as good a state as we found it. Moreover, it's also compatible with the 'light at the end of the tunnel' perspective, which is after all the ultimate 'happily ever after.

In fact, it seems to me that, whatever our final destination, walking with the dark man can help us all feel happier, safer, more satisfied and contented. It can help us look to the darkness and light with equal equanimity and enjoy both for their similar-ities and their differences. It can help us live in peace with ourselves and our world, and, by extension, with the rest of the world. It can help create a world of balance, trust, adventure, tolerance and love. And maybe, if we work towards all this on a day-to-day basis, the eventual outcome will arrive by itself – maybe, but, as always, you'll have to make up your own mind about these things. To finish, though, I'd like to leave you with a quote by the guitarist Ron Thal, who, regardless of what in heaven or earth he dreams of in his own philosophy, sums things up pretty nicely for us here.

I'm a believer in hard work and being focussed. I figure that if I can do it, anyone can! Seriously, just put your mind to things, have faith, patience, trust and good things will happen.

There's an endless road of things I can't do...There's an endless amount of growing and learning, and there's always more. Don't forget it. The day you stop learning is the day you start sucking. My days are numbered. I'm just trying to get as far down the road as I can.[1]

Thanks for reading.
Enjoy the journey.
Debbie xx

Notes

Introduction

1   Jung, C.G. (1927) 'Psychological Commentary' (Hull, R.F.C. trans.) in Evans-Wentz, W.Y. (ed.) (1927/1960) *The Tibetan Book of the Dead*, Oxford, Oxford University Press, p. xlvi.

Chapter 1: The Dark Man

1   Campbell, J. (1949) *The Hero with a Thousand Faces*, London, Fontana Press, pp. 51–6.

2   Graves, R. (1948/1952) Lindop, G. (ed.) *The White Goddess*, London, Faber and Faber, p. 20.

3   *Ibid.* p. 20.

4   *Ibid.* p. 5.

5   *Ibid.* p. 20.

6   Campbell, J. (1949) *The Hero with a Thousand Faces*, London, Fontana Press, pp. 118–9.

7   Estés, C.P. (1992) *Women Who Run with the Wolves*, London, Rider, p. 39.

8   *Ibid.* p. 66.

9   *Ibid.* pp. 70–1.

10 In a materialistic model of the universe matter is the fundamental substance of all things – including mind. Yet, while this view is the current scientific orthodoxy, it is worth noting that scientists, philosophers and theologians have been wrangling for centuries about the problem of mind and (whatever *anyone* may say to the contrary) they still don't know how it works, what it is, or whether mind or matter (or even mind *and* matter) is the fundamental stuff out of which everything else is made.

11 Jung, C.G. (1927) 'Psychological Commentary' (Hull, R.F.C. trans.) in Evans-Wentz, W.Y. (ed.) (1927/1960) *The Tibetan Book of the Dead*, Oxford, Oxford University Press.

12   *Ibid.* p. xliv.

13   *Ibid.* p. xlv.

14   Admittedly, there are philosophical theses which claim that this might not be the case, but for the sake of argument I am choosing to set these aside. Yet, for anyone who might be interested in these ideas, Descartes' *Meditations on First Philosophy* would be a good place to start.

15   This is not a problem, however, if we agree with the 'Eastern' view of the mind (see below).

16   A third position, known as *dualism*, which holds that both mind *and* matter are the fundamental substances of all things, is also possible. Descartes forwarded this theory in his *Meditations of First Philosophy*, but nowadays it is largely (and perhaps unfairly) dismissed.

17   *Ibid.* p. xliii.

18   *Ibid.* pp. xliii–xliv.

19   *Ibid.* p. lii.

Chapter 2: Meeting the Dark Man

1   Graves, R. (1948/1952) Lindop, G. (ed.) *The White Goddess*, London, Faber and Faber, p. 20.

2   Smith, D.M. Leicester, S. (1996) *Hug the Monster*, London, Rider, pp. xiv–xv.

3   It does seem, though, as if 3.00am may have replaced midnight as the 'witching hour', at least here in the West, where electric lighting, heating and round-the-clock 'entertainment' may have knocked our natural rhythms out of kilter.

4   Estés, C.P. (1992) *Women Who Run with the Wolves*, London, Rider, p. 48.

5   *Ibid.*

6   Carter, A. (1979) 'The Company of Wolves' in Zipes, J. (ed.) (1993) *The Trials and Tribulations of Little Red Riding Hood*, London, Routledge, p. 289.

7   For example, what you were doing/thinking at the time; what was happening in your life; how you knew it was the dark man; what he looked like; what (if any) associates were with him; what happened, and so on.

8   Estés, C.P. (1992) *Women Who Run With the Wolves*, London, Rider, p. 39.

9   This is *very often* experienced as a faulty telephone, an inability to key numbers into a telephone, or as the inability or unwillingness of other people to hear what we have to say.

10 Note the motif of the bridge, or to be more precise the 'sword bridge', which appears in various legendary tales.

11 There are numerous dark man motifs in this dream including the door, the secret room, and the filth or excrement. And it is also worth noting the close parallels to the story 'Bluebeard' when the young wife discovers the killing room.

12 Again there are a number of dark man motifs in this dream, including the entrance to an underground passage, a 'door' (which in this case was a web, curtain or veil), darkness and death. And again, there are strong similarities between this dream and the discovery of Bluebeard's killing room.

13 Note the parallels with Ruth's dream and with Robert Graves' 'Prince of the Air'.

14 Grandma died about three weeks later.

15 You may remember that the term 'bogeyman' means 'hobgoblin'.

16 Estés, C.P. (1992) *Women Who Run with the Wolves*, London, Rider, p. 68.

Chapter 3: The Underworld

1   For example, when the Olympian gods Hades, Poseidon and Zeus drew straws to decide who would preside over which domain, Zeus became the God of Heaven, Poseidon became the God of the Sea, and Hades drew the short straw to become the God of the Underworld. Similarly, when the

fallen angels 'lay with the daughters of men' and taught 'men' the skills of metallurgy, sorcery, astronomy, etc. the angels were bound to earth as punishment (Enoch 7 – 13); in Revelation 'the beast' was chained and locked into a bottomless pit for one thousand years (Revelation 20); and in the story of *Beauty and the Beast* the prince was transformed into a hideous beast until the day love restored his true form.

2   In separating the Otherworld in this way people are simply dividing a substantial and profound *whole* into smaller, more workable *chunks*, and other divisions such as *trinities* and *pantheons of twelve* are also common. Nevertheless, even when the Otherworld is split along these more complex lines, the basic light–dark division almost always remains intact.

3   This division reflects the fundamentals of biology and not the politics of sociology, and the facts are that 'the masculine' *projects* while 'the feminine' *receives*, and the same holds true whether we are talking about flowers, bumble bees, blue tits or human beings. What's more, the 'rationality' ascribed to the masculine is simply an effect of being in *the light*, while the 'intuitiveness and mystery' of the feminine reflects the condition of *darkness* as well as the mysterious processes that occur deep within a woman as she creates new life.

4   It may be a good thing that we can't see these things in their true form, for when Zeus's lover, the mortal Semele, demanded that Zeus reveal himself to her in his true nature, she was instantly consumed by his lightning and thunderbolts. Her mortal mind and body just couldn't tolerate what she saw.

5   Though if you believe that mind is a product of matter then any effects will still have to wait for atoms, molecules, and so on, to shuffle around.

6   Masaru Emoto's water crystal photographs reveal how rapidly water molecules can respond, e.g. Emoto, M. (2004) *The Hidden Messages in Water*, Hillsboro, Beyond Words

Publishing Inc.

7 This idea sits quite happily with the *law of nature* and *old god* views of the Otherworld, but not so well with the notion that it is 'all in the mind', unless, that is, all individual minds are identical (which is unlikely and cannot explain how some group experiences occur) and/or interconnected.

8 Remember that laws of nature/old gods/archetypes are initially devoid of content (i.e. invisible to us) until they become 'coloured' by appropriate images and experiences from our everyday life.

9 This does not mean that every particular story, dream, mystical, religious, shamanistic and psychological tradition wholly concurs with one other and with the outline of the Underworld presented here. But what it does mean is that when you look at these various areas and disciplines a broad pattern emerges, and it is this pattern – this broad model of understanding – that I hold to be representative of the Underworldly landscape.

10 This depends on the story or the model of the Otherworld/Cosmos employed.

11 The Otherworld underlies and shapes all things, and the Theme is the story of the Otherworld. Thus all 'true' stories, poems, etc. are in fact telling the story of creation, or of *continuing creation*, or of *continuing creation that carries on giving shape to all that we know*. This is why poets and story-tellers were once revered and feared, as it was believed that, through their knowledge of the Otherworld and the words they used, they had had the ability to affect (for good or for evil) the fabric of creation. One had to be very careful not to cross such people!

12 Incidentally, being **re-clothed** in some way, usually in garments of sky-blue, silver, or silver-white, or in clothes covered in sparkling jewels or mirrors, is a symbol that commonly occurs at this point on the path.

13 I am not just talking about mystics, shamans, etc. here, as some psychologists work with the archetypal contents of the human mind, some scientists work with laws of nature, and many other people work with the hunches and insights they receive through their dreams, daydreams, etc. even though they often have no idea what they are actually experiencing.

14 Traditions that split the Otherworld on a vertical axis (◐) often saw the entrance to the Underworld as being in the cold, dark **North** and its exit in the brighter, warmer **South**, while those who split the Otherworld horizontally (◑) often held that its entrance was in the **West** (the place of the setting sun or the gateway into darkness) and that its exit was in the **East** (the place where the sun is reborn).

15 It doesn't take a huge amount of imagination to envisage that everything in nature is kept pootling along by the effect of natural laws (old gods) exerting their influence on things, or *shepherding* them along.

Chapter 4: The Lord of the Underworld

1 There is another theory which suggests that all our memories and experiences are held in some kind of *group mind*. Some call this 'Akasha', others the 'Collective Unconscious', and some see it as a kind of cultural or familial legacy. But whatever we choose to call it, the idea remains that the fears and limitations we face today are not just those surrounding our own personal problems and issues, but are those which have beleaguered our ancestors, our society, our culture, humanity or possibly even all of creation since the beginning of time.

2 Campbell, J. (1949) *The Hero with a Thousand Faces*, London, Fontana Press, p. 53.

3 Pseudonym.

4 As with the dark man, the way that we perceive Desire is necessarily coloured by our actions and attitudes towards

him. So if we have a reasonably healthy relationship with this god/law/archetype, then we will experience him as a light, bright, positive entity/energy. However, if our relationship with him is distorted, then he will take on a darker, more sinister form that is not so pleasant to live with.

5   There is the issue of Desire being a *masculine* deity. Very briefly, Desire is a masculine entity only insofar as he originates from the light, projective, masculine side of the Otherworld. In fact, Desire is best thought of as androgynous, belonging to either sex, or as passion personified. For example, in myth *Apollo* was equally attractive to men and women and took lovers of both sexes. Similarly, *gold* is desired by men and women, though traditionally (or stereotypically) men and women have valued the precious metal for different reasons.

6   Hence the traditional fear of solar eclipses.

7   The dark man following on from desire is what lies behind the famous 'pact with the Devil' storyline.

8   Three questions you might ask yourself in readiness for this time are: *What is it I really want? What stands in my way? How far am I prepared to go for my heart's desire?*

9   In traditional tales these resources are often represented as the rations the seeker carries in his or her bundle, as a weapon, a piece of armour, or a *magical item* that is found, won or given to the seeker at the beginning of the quest.

10 Ruth, from chapter 2, could have taken either of these options, but instead she bolted at the sight of the dark man and, as far as I know, has never allowed herself to be moved by desire since.

11 Pseudonym.

12 For instance:
Come to the edge.
We might fall.
Come to the edge.

It's too high!
COME TO THE EDGE!
And they came
And he pushed them
And they flew.

Christopher Logue (English poet 1926-)

Come to the Edge (originally titled *Apollinaire Said*) is a beautiful poem. However, we shouldn't be so naïve as to assume that in real life we can simply skip towards our dreams, goals and ambitions and have everything fall miraculously into place. Yes, it *can* happen. But what usually *does* happen is that the moment we step off of the edge we fall into a nose-dive and maybe even crash and burn, whereupon the real issue becomes *'What the hell do we do now!?'* for the door into the Underworld only swings one way, so once we've taken that step into the unknown there is *no* going back.

13 Significantly, there is little doubt that there is a dark feminine presence within the masculine centre of the light side of the Otherworld. And this female-in-male, as well as a male-in-female, presence is precisely what is depicted in the yin–yang symbol☯.

14 Estés, C.P. (1992) *Women Who Run with the Wolves*, London, Rider, pp. 415–416.

15 In Grandma's case, she dreamed that the inhospitable land was *Texas*, which was a strange and faraway land to her. And although Texas isn't cold and stark, from watching old films Grandma did believe it to be an arid, barren environment.

16 This does depend upon your understanding of the word 'forever'. If you hold that forever is the space of one lifetime, then it is quite possible for a person to remain in a condition of darkness, confusion, loneliness and despair until the very end. However, if you believe that death is just a passing and that the cycle continues, then sooner or later even the most lost of souls will eventually 'see the light'.

17 Hill, N. (1937/2003) *Think and Grow Rich*, London, Vermillion. p. 251.

18 The Sumerian goddess of love Inanna is said to have descended into the Underworld to attend the funeral of the husband of her sister Ereshkigal. Yet the gatekeeper stopped Inanna at each of the seven gates into the Underworld and demanded that she remove a piece of her clothing, until, naked, Inanna reached the centre of the Underworld and stood before Ereshkigal (the goddess of the Underworld), who announced that Inanna must now die and that her body must be hung from a stake. Inanna was eventually released, however, and returned to the land of the living, while her own husband, who had celebrated when he thought she was dead, had to take her place in the Land of the Dead.

19 Though at higher levels of mysticism mind, time and being are held to be the same thing.

20 This reflects, in part, the disagreement over the extent of the role the dark man has within the Underworld.

21 This represents the waning crescent moon, no moon and the waxing crescent moon; which in turn represents the three aspects of the triple goddess, and/or the tripartite natures of the maiden, mother and crone.

22 Granny's cottage, the gingerbread house, a castle or a tall tower are all familiar fairytale examples.

23 A second interpretation is that the first crescent corresponds to the entrance into the underworld, the dot to its abyssal heart, and the second crescent to the far gate. However, these two interpretations are not in conflict, as the second is simply taking a wider view, while the one we are concentrating on here looks at the unicorn's eye from a tighter perspective.

24 This arch is often seen to be shaped by two or more overreaching trees, traditionally of either pear or aspen.

25 As was the serpent in Hera's Garden of the Hesperides.

26 As was Beast in *Beauty and the Beast*, the bear in *Snow White*

and Rose Red or even the serpent in the *Garden of Eden* (though it is possible that this serpent was, in fact, female).

27 Frogs rarely turn into princes and 'love's first kiss' isn't a peck on the cheek. You see, it is never about *sanitising* or *elevating* the dark man; it's about us *getting down* in the dirt.

28 When I said in chapter 2 that the dark man is never an object of desire, I was telling the truth (mostly), for while the divine marriage certainly involves a union of sorts, it is one that is based on respect and trust and not steaming-hot, fiery-pants desire.

29 If you are male, remember that what is being talked about here are the 'female' qualities of humility and grace, or the surrender of our wilful, egotistical and intellectual encumbrances to 'that which is greater than ourselves'. Admittedly, the imagery of your dreams, etc. may differ from these classic fairytale interpretations – for instance, you may eat with the guardian (bread or meat are common symbols) or drink from his cup (wine, water or beer are frequent) before falling into a deep sleep – but the message remains the same.

30 As marked by the dot between the two crescents: ☾•☽.

31 Or some other symbol which is associated with the preparation or presentation of food.

32 Again, please remember that 'the maiden' represents a state of being rather than actual gender.

33 The alternative to our returning in this way would be to live out our days as a wraith in the land of the dead.

34 Think of the film *Groundhog Day*. In it 'Phil' experiences countless 'false starts' until he eventually develops the grace and humility to pass through the centre and experience his tomorrow.

35 Typically three, five, seven, nine or one hundred pieces.

36 This is probably the single most mystical idea presented in this book, and it is one that is found at the core of many religious and spiritual ideologies (though the dark man's role

is not always explicitly stated), and it has the potential to stir up a number of interesting corollaries concerning, amongst other things, theology, the nature of creation, time, reincarnation and life's purpose. However, please don't worry if you're having difficulty getting your head around the concept (it is, after all, an inscrutable mystery to most people); instead simply think that in the context of what we are talking about here (a) the old mother *stacked fate* to give you the potential to arrive at your heart's desire, while (b) the seed of creation you carry within you is *the seed of your new life* – whatever that may mean to you.

37 Those who have legitimately entered the Underworld at the behest of 'the gods'; who have diligently stuck to their quest; who have surrendered to the divine marriage and passed through the unicorn's eye, these people will graciously be allowed to leave the Underworld when they arrive at the final gate. However, anyone who has entered without permission, and who has stolen from the gods (in myth this is sometimes portrayed as 'fire theft'), will either have to fight their way out of the darkness (and it is questionable whether this is possible) or pray to be rescued from without.

38 And I do mean *suddenly*, for once we have passed through the centre, things that we might have been working on for ages can abruptly and *out of the blue* fall into place. They say 'What a difference a day makes!' and, at this time, our life can literally be turned around in days, hours or even minutes – it really is as though a fairy's wand has been waved over our head.

39 Campbell, J. (1949) *The Hero with a Thousand Faces*, London, Fontana Press, p. 218.

40 The price for this is to surrender all hope, desire, family, home, sunshine and beautiful, precious life.

41 In many cases these changes are quite subtle, but occasionally they can be so profound it is as though a whole new person

has emerged.

42 It is sometimes referred to as *paradise* or *bliss*.

43 The fall from fulfilment to discontent being the story of the light side of the Otherworld.

44 For instance, I don't believe it is 'right' to impose on, or manipulate, another person's free will. And although this statement opens up a philosophical minefield, I think that most people would agree that it would be pretty undesirable to live in a universe within which we could be forced to acquiesce to other people's desires. This said, there are *many* people who hold that such 'low magic' is both acceptable and practicable... though this is a subject that falls way outside the scope of this book.

45 Trying to work out the reasons for anyone's actions involves a degree of speculation and imprecision, but when we start trying to second-guess *old gods* the problem increases exponentially!

46 By whatever name he has been known by.

47 Many hold that in the *very* beginning there was nothing or non-being, which some called *Chaos* and others referred to as the *Waters of the Abyss* or the *Primal Void*, and that the original entity known as 'God', etc. emerged from this state of nothingness.

48 *In the beginning God created the heaven and the earth. And the earth was without form, and void; and darkness was upon the face of the deep. And the Spirit of God moved upon the face of the waters.*

And God said, Let there be light: and there was light.

And God saw the light, that it was good: and God divided the light from the darkness.

Genesis1:1–4 King James Version (KJV)

49 *Then the voices of the Ainur, like unto harps and lutes, and pipes and trumpets, and viols and organs, and like unto countless choirs singing with words, began to fashion the theme of Ilúvatar [God]*

to a great music; and a sound arose of endless interchanging melodies woven in harmony that passed beyond hearing into the depths and into the heights, and the places of the dwelling of Ilúvatar were filled to overflowing, and the music and the echo of the music went out into the Void, and it was not void. Tolkein, J.R.R. (1977) *Silmarillion*, London, Harper Collins, pp. 3–4.

50 Laurence, R. (trans.) in Prophet, E.C. (1983/1992) *Forbidden Mysteries of Enoch: Fallen Angels and the Origins of Evil*, Corwin Springs, Summit University Press, pp. 92–95.

51 Revelation 20:1–3 KJV.

52 Revelation 20:10 KJV.

53 2 Peter 2:4 KJV.

54 Jude 6 KJV.

55 There is an old saying: *Hell's on Earth and Heaven's what you make it.*

56 As we saw in chapter 3, mortal men and women are comprised of both light and dark, or 'masculine' and 'feminine' attributes. However, whether it is down to nature or nurture, women on the whole tend to live by more of their feminine qualities than do men.

57 Laurence, R. (trans.) in Prophet, E.C. (1983/1992) *Forbidden Mysteries of Enoch: Fallen Angels and the Origins of Evil*, Corwin Springs, Summit University Press, pp. 92–93 (Enoch 7:1–7).

58 *Ibid.* pp. 104–105.

59 *Ibid.* p. 94 (Enoch 8:1) and pp. 97–100 (Enoch 10:12; 13:1–3).

60 Again, 'evil' isn't inherent within any of these skills. Instead, evil is in the purpose to which some human beings choose to put their efforts and knowledge.

Chapter 5: Introducing... Us

1 Or of our *mind* and our *perceptions* of our world.

2 Note, though, that as you make your way through the darkness and things begin to change, it is natural that some

old soul groups will fall away and new interests and passions will develop.

3 This response isn't only used by those who are lost and afraid in the Underworld; however, it is a *very common* reaction to this situation.

4 And not all stressful changes and choices are 'bad'. For example, according to Washington University 'stress experts' Thomas Holmes and Richard Hale, getting married is moderately more stressful than losing your job, which itself is only slightly more stressful than retirement, pregnancy or the death of a close friend.

5 This technique was adapted from the book *Healing Mind, Healthy Woman* (1996, Thorsons), in which *Dr Alice Domar and Henry Dreher* comprehensively explain the effects that stress can have on our health and well-being, and offer various ways of handling the problem, naturally. They call these techniques 'Mini-Relaxations', or 'the perfect portable stress managers'.

6 Or, alternatively, those who just moan and gripe about what they have or have not got, while doing *absolutely nothing* to put things right.

7 Baum, L.F. (1900, 1993) *The Wizard of Oz*, Ware, Wordsworth Editions Limited, pp. 52–53.

8 Estés, C.P. (1992) *Women Who Run with the Wolves*, London, Rider, p. 319.

9 Some would say that the whole point of the journey through the Underworld is to liberate ourselves from both our darkness *and* our desires – but that is another story.

10 Code, K. (1983, 2002) *A Twist of the Wrist*, California, Code Break Inc., p. 54.

11 *Ibid.*

12 *Ibid.* p. 58.

13 Dyer, W.W. (1997) *Manifest your Destiny*, London, Thorsons, pp. 62–63.

14 Or talk and *think*, for that matter.

15 Estés, C.P. (1992) *Women Who Run With the Wolves*, London, Rider, p. 59.

16 As we have seen, you can think of this higher power as your 'unconscious' or your 'instinct or intuition'; you can think of it as 'the balance of nature'; or you can understand it to be some higher 'external consciousness' or 'old god'. In this book we refer to this energy as 'the dark man'. However, please remember that it doesn't really matter how you understand it or what name you choose to give it; what really matters is that you recognise this power as a real and imperative force that is at the centre of your own life.

17 'Harry Lime' from the screenplay *The Third Man*, by Graham Green.

18 Cornfield, J. (1994) *A Path With a Heart*, London, Rider, pp. 14–15.

19 *Ibid.* p. 14.

20 It is important to realise that making a mess of things on a personal level does not necessarily mean that we have fouled things up archetypally. Yet the reverse is not true, for if we do manage to mess up the archetypal flow of life, this will almost certainly have a negative effect on our day to day health, happiness and well-being.

Chapter 6: When It Goes Wrong

1 Or 'cycles within cycles' or 'wheels within wheels'.

2 Or 'helix'.

3 And it is important to note here that our ancestors were not merely ignorant natives who fabricated stories in the absence of scientific facts. On the contrary, the tales they told and the old gods who populated these tales were sophisticated representations, *using the concepts and words available to them at the time,* of natural forces, and the interplay between these natural forces, that modern science cannot even begin to

explain today! Maybe one day science will catch up. But even so, it will still only be telling the same story in yet another language and from yet another standpoint. And all the while the cycle of life will grind onwards.

4   An idolised deity is very different from an 'old god', at least as it is seen here, for an old god is a demiurge, or one of the fundamental 'makers and shapers' of creation, which is why we can say that the only difference between an old god and a blind law of nature is that the old god has conscious intent. In contrast, an idolised deity is taken 'out of the workplace', plonked on a lofty perch, fed grapes and nectar, and suppli- cated by servile minions who hope to gain his favour – or at least avoid his wrath.

5   As we have seen, alcohol, sex, TV, shopping, etc. can also be (and often are) used as toxic distractions from the real world.

6   Mayne, B. (2006) *Goal Mapping*, London, Watkins, p. 89.

7   Incidentally, as the darkness becomes darker, so the light side of the Otherworld (i.e. our everyday world) becomes increas- ingly distorted, swollen, demanding and rapacious, and things become harder and harder to achieve as we are always trying to have/do bigger and 'better' things within a smaller, uglier reality.

8   Remember, *the divine marriage* is a moment of trust and surrender, and not a time of gooey romance or hot desire.

Conclusion: Walking with the Dark Man

1   Thal, R. in Yates, H. (2009) 'Guns N' Roses', *Total Guitar*, 184, pp. 66–68.

BOOKS

O is a symbol of the world, of oneness and unity. In different cultures it also means the "eye," symbolizing knowledge and insight. We aim to publish books that are accessible, constructive and that challenge accepted opinion, both that of academia and the "moral majority."

Our books are available in all good English language bookstores worldwide. If you don't see the book on the shelves ask the bookstore to order it for you, quoting the ISBN number and title. Alternatively you can order online (all major online retail sites carry our titles) or contact the distributor in the relevant country, listed on the copyright page.

See our website **www.o-books.net** for a full list of over 500 titles, growing by 100 a year.

And tune in to myspiritradio.com for our book review radio show, hosted by June-Elleni Laine, where you can listen to the authors discussing their books.

mySpiRitRaдio